Liggia!

I WAS BLESSED
WITH ANGELS

Congrats!

Love,

I WAS BLESSED
WITH ANGELS

Tamia Bethea Williams Story

TAMIA BETHEA WILLIAMS

RW&D
PUBLISHING

TAYLOR, MICHIGAN

I Was Blessed With Angels
Tamia Bethea Williams Story

Copyright © 2018 by Tamia Bethea Williams

Published by RW&D Publishing

13161 Golf Pointe Drive
Taylor, Michigan 48180
904-540-2894

First Printing, First Edition 2018.

Publisher: RW&D Publishing 2018.

Caution: All rights reserved.

Tamia Bethea Williams, Multi-Level Marketing Professional
and Trainer.

ISBN: 978-1-64136-427-0

Printed in USA.

Publisher and Editor: John Howard Jr. Ph.D. – Owner RW&D
Publishing

Cover Design by Jera Publishing

Publisher's Note:

This story is a Biographical Sketch.

Books are available for quantity discount when used for promotion,
production or services. Contact Tamia Bethea Williams.

Voices from the Sky

"Tamia has the secret sauce for transformation. The way she combines her life experience, her gift for teaching, her humor, and her ability to connect with anyone as a mentor and a friend, this is how she will shake you up and turn you inside out and right side up and you will never be the same again."

- Lily Tyson, Alkaline Nation USA Holyoke, Massachusetts

"This is a fabulous book about a humble woman who has had so many obstacles and adversities in her life. But still she rises. Tamia is a great inspiration to so many people. People can heal their life by reading this book. "I Was Blessed With Angels" is a true gift to anyone looking for hope, support, and miracles in living their passion."

- Jennifer Jones Mahgoub, Albrightsville, PA

"Tamia, is a living testimony that proves trials are only a Test, to discover the Testimony!' She has been a wonderful influence in my life as a Leader and Friend. One of my favorite quotes from Tamia is, 'We don't go through situations, instead we Grow through them.'"

- Monique Washington, Author, Entrepreneur, California

"There are certain people that come into your life who make such an impact, who leave such an indelible mark, that your life is truly changed forever. Tamia Bethea Williams is one such person. To see her today, to know her as she appears to the world right now, paints just the result of a life fully experienced. To know her is to know her story, where she began, the struggles, trials and tribulations she has grown through. But as is Tamia's spirit, she didn't stop there. She took her life lessons, the bumps, bruises, and scars, and made them into something truly remarkable to share with others. This book is her story, or we should say, the beginning of her story, as it is still being written for the blessings of us all."

- Carl Carvalho and Caroline Gavin, Certified Trainers & Life and Business Coaches, New Jersey

"This book eliminates guessing. Even if you just started the business, people want to follow you because of your knowledge and excellent guidelines. It makes life easy and duplicatable. I got 100 of your training books and exploded my business. Thank you, daughter Tamia; you are a God sent!"

- Tita Franco, Batac City Ilocos Norte Philippines

"Tamia Bethea Williams is down to earth and humble—yet bold and courageous. She is forever inspiring others to grow and to become all that they can be. From rags to riches, Tamia has seen it all and she continues to soar in her leadership and in her faith while she freely shares her life lessons with the world. Her book may be titled I Was Blessed With Angels," but it's my life that has been blessed by this angel!"

- Lynn Gardner, Advocate and Author, Washington, DC

"Tamia's story is a roller coaster ride inside the challenges and rewards of parenting a child with a chronic developmental disability. It is a journey from discouragement to encouragement, from despair to hope, and from frustrations to enriching revelations.

Tamia, then, is the ambassador beckoning millions of families with special needs members. Hers is a demonstrative call to step out of the closet to embrace the support, hope, empowerment, and bliss awaiting them and their angels, as they connect in a renewed and inspiring way with society."

- R. Malika Owusu-Hassan, M.Ed., Licensed School Psychologist, Ret

"It's extremely rare to encounter someone who makes such a dramatically positive impact on you that the trajectory of your life is changed forever. Tamia Williams is that person

Tamia draws on her own life experience to relay energy that is simply amazing. Transfusing that energy into others has become a passion and an area of expertise for Ms. Williams. This book is sure to have the same effect.

Grounded in humble beginnings, for the last 30 years Tamia has poured her life out for others bettering, her students in Public School, business mentees in numerous organizations, and marketing leaders across the globe.

"I Was Blessed With Angels" chronicles Tamia's story. As you read this incredible journey, you will also realize the Tamia herself has been an angel to countless numbers of people. I am one of the thousands in that number."

- Henry Howell, Madison Avenue Advertising Veteran

"Nowadays, it is not easy to find someone who I enjoy collaborating.

It is rare to meet someone who would understand all aspects from corporate philosophy, company's mission to true leadership. It is far rare to find someone who would also swell positive energy and good charisma.

Whenever this lady enters the room, the room would immediately power up, the energy would evolve instantly, only her beautiful story would be shared. The name of this lady, this special person, is Tamia! I am honored to meet her, to know her, to collaborate with her!

"Only a few things in life are really important." This simple philosophy may touch many by heart, but may not necessarily reach their souls.

"Change your present," "Own your dream," "Draw out the blueprint of your future, ... For those who want to own their dreams, drive their destinies, but still take no action after many encouragements from others, I recommend this book to you! I am sure after they read this book, they will realize, "What's their promise to their future?" I believe this book holds this special power!"

- KATSUMASA ISOBE

Contents

"I acknowledge
all the "Angels" that
made this publication possible!"

Dedication

I want to thank my Grandma and Granddad, Essie and Earlie Bethea! I am so happy and grateful that you took the time to take care of me when I didn't even know myself. You taught me right from wrong before I could write my name. Although I didn't understand your reasons for saying and doing some of the things you said and did, because of you, I learned to follow my dreams and become a positive role model for others to follow. From you, I learned the importance of honesty and arduous work to achieve my goals. I am who I am today because of you. I miss you, and I love you very much; I am forever grateful for the life lessons you taught me, and I will never forget you.

I want to thank my Mom and Dad, Sharon and Willie Bethea! I am so happy and grateful that you created and kept me in your lives. From you mom, I learned to love my children and grandchildren like I love myself. I realize that caring for me and dealing with the challenges of raising a child in the South while handling the demands of your own personal affairs could often be overwhelming.

Because of you dad, I learned patience, kindness, and understanding. I thank you for always being there for me whether I was wrong or right. I thank you for supporting me. Although at times we had different opinions, our divergent views allowed us both to grow. I will always remember your favorite words "It's just a feeling. It will soon pass." I now understand that emotions are just those feelings that will soon pass away. I never conceded to personal issues which we may have encountered; my thinking is broader, and my skin is thicker because of our differences Thank you for teaching me that.

Although life was difficult and raising me was not an easy experience for either one of you, I can proudly say that both of you did it successfully with love and compassion.

Thank you Shavon, Damian, and Shantel, my children and Jaylen, Jeremy, and Cyia, my grandchildren! All of you mean the world to me. You are extensions of me, and I love you from my entire heart not just the bottom. You are the reasons I do what I do. I am so proud of each one of you.

Each of you is different in your own way, and I have been blessed to watch you grow and develop into amazing human beings! Shavon, we have come a long way: we matured from showing little affection for one another to never hanging up without saying I love you or never walking away without sharing a hug. I have watched you struggle and succeed at the same time. You are an amazing young lady, and I know your best is yet to come. The sky is the limit; keep your head high and proud because you are a winner.

Damian, I am so happy you came into my life. Because of you, I have learned how to love stronger. You have taught me more than you will ever know. Because of you, I have super compassion my awesome son. They said you would never do a lot of things, but GOD look at you now. I wouldn't trade you for no one. I am privileged to be your mother! Shantel, life hasn't always been easy, but you are one strong cookie. You arrived as an old soul because you have always been very mature! I have watched you navigate through many obstacles, yet you still prevailed! Your smile is electrifying; you are adored by many. Stay focused, and you will be able to be, do, and have whatever you so desire!

Thank You Tony my life Partner! I know what it means to find a soulmate. Because you listen to your heart, I now listen to mine. You are the man I mentally designed and always dreamed of years before you ambled onto my stage of life. Because I waited, and didn't look or force a relationship, you appeared when I least expected. Now I understand what it means when people say, "Good Things Come to Those Who Wait." I feel so blessed to have you; you are my best friend, my counselor, my spiritual partner, my better half all bundled into "One Sweet Package." Today we share a love that most only hope for in a lifetime. I thank Jehovah for you every day. I feel like I have known you my entire life. You make me better, and I am grateful.

Finally, to my business partners, I am thankful for you also. I would never leave you out of my story. Because of you, my story grows and survives. Imagine an organization filled with excitement all the time, embodied with millions of personal characteristics that interact in positive ways every day. I continue to enjoy every moment of my chosen profession. I have watched my partners evolve into amazing trainers, leaders, teachers, coaches, top earners, and speakers. All of you have helped me in more ways than you can imagine. You have stretched my mind and abilities; I am a better leader because of you. I humbly thank you. I love you.

All of you are my Angels!
Tamia Bethea Williams

"I went with these men who
I didn't know to unfamiliar
places to work in a vegetable
field away from home."

My Mother's Parents

MY JOURNEY BEGAN in Latta, South Carolina on October 28th, 1968 to the parents of Sharon and Willie Bethea. My father literally had to ask my grandparents, Essie and Earlie Bethea to marry my mother because she was too young to get married. She was 16 years old when she married my dad and 17 years old when she gave birth to me.

Because of personal challenges in the marriage, my grandparents raised me. From the time I knew my grandparents, they were always hard-working people. For my grandparents, I know I was a challenge for them because they had already raised 11 children of their own as well as a few grandchildren. My great-grand mother, birthed 11 children also, including my grandmother. My great-grand mother was an alcoholic; she passed away before having the opportunity to raise all of her own children. As a result, my

> "The lack of affection was like a disease in my house."

grandmother ended up raising her own siblings. She had already done her share of raising children and then I came along — this beautiful bouncing baby girl.

My grandfather and grandmother took over raising me when I was very young. They were the only parents I really knew for a very long time. My grandmother often referred to me as being a motherless and fatherless child. You will soon understand why.

Grandfather, Earlie Bethea

Grandfather Earlie was a sharecropper. He taught me a lot about planting. This man could grow anything, anywhere. Grandpa Earlie was not a religious zealot but a down-home church-man, proud to serve his Lord and Savior and God fearing. Every "Good Friday," my grandfather seeded his garden. If I didn't know any better, I would have thought that he planted the Garden of Eden.

Regardless of the weather or circumstance, every year, he planted corn, okra, peas, tomatoes, squash, cucumbers, watermelon, cantaloupe, rotating them when needed. My job was easy. He dug the hole, and I placed the seeds in the hole then I covered the hole with moist dirt.

We had several caterpillar trees. He taught me how to catch the caterpillars and put them in a can. He used them as bate every year to catch eels, catfish and turtles. I loved the way grandma prepared turtle meat. Everyone on Henry Street and Charles Street loved the way she prepared turtle meat also. Preparing and cooking turtle meat was a very tedious process, but the final product was worth the wait! My grandmother would make several pans of turtle meat then give most of it away. The way she prepared the turtle meat; she made it tasted the same each time. It was always delicious. I can smell it now and taste it to. Today, I sure wish I could duplicate her method the way she used to.

Everybody knew, my grandfather, Mr. Earlie. Many people were afraid of my grandfather too. I wasn't. My grandfather was a very tall dark man with steel-grey eyes. He had a voice that commanded attention, broad and beaming. I think I inherited that quality of speaking from him now that I think about it. He was a no-nonsense person. He was well respected in our town.

My grandfather and I were very close. He displayed an almost contradictory form of discipline, often chastising me then rewarding me with a treat, my favorite lollypop. He rewarded my inappropriate behavior. He was easy to love as far as I was concerned. To me, he was the apple of my eye.

I could get my grandfather to give me anything I wanted. Some people would say, I had him twisted around my little tiny fingers. I like to believe that we were intertwined. My grandmother knew this as well. She knew how to take advantage of our relationship. I could get my granddad to do things for her as well. One day I watched my grandfather sign his check. He placed a big (X) on the back. I asked him why he did that. He confided in me. He could not write his name. The bank accepted an X as his signature. He had a

3

first-grade education. I was shocked, surprised by the event, confused because my grandpa excelled in mathematics. He could count every dime in the bank.

He performed many demanding chores, but he couldn't read or write. Because of this, I made a commitment to help my grandfather write his name. We started practicing hand over hand to teach him how to write his name. Picture my little hands on top of my grandfather's huge hands showing him how to write his name. He learned how to do it. He learned how to write his name. We were so excited. Because he was excited, I was over joyed with his accomplishment, for the first time watching him write his name in print and eventually in script.

We had accomplished something together that I initiated rather than an activity which he started. I didn't give up on him, like he never gave up on me. I was determined to help him, and I did. He started signing the back of his checks, Earlie Bethea. My grandmother said, "I should become a teacher." She was very prophetic, indeed.

My grandfather was an excellent fisherman. I went fishing with him often, enjoying our moments of solitude, sitting on the river bank with our crude wooden fishing sticks in hand, dangling the homemade twine and penny hooks in the water, relaxing as the slow-moving current rippled against the line while the plastic bobber floated gently up and down with each rising and falling wave.

I just enjoyed being with my grandfather. When he was sick, he promised to take me fishing again; however, he died right after my fourteenth birthday. I was angry with him for many years for not fulfilling his promise. I felt like death was a choice not an evolutionary fact. I believed people could control how long they stayed here on earth, and they had the power to decide when they would leave. It's amazing how I thought back then.

My grandfather died due to poor health. He succumbed to complications involving diabetes. The diabetes affected his mind as well. Sometimes he did some strange things like putting his shirt in the refrigerator thinking it was the closet. I wish I knew then what I know now about the human body. I believe he would not have suffered so much for so long.

When people asked who my father was, I would say my grandfather. I didn't want to add more to my emotional plate.

Grandmother, Essie Bethea

I feel that this part of my life is what really helped to shape and mold me into who I am today. I believe this is the definition of who Tamia really is and has become. My grandmother went the extra mile for me because to her I was a motherless and a fatherless child. I heard her say that often. She wanted the best for me, and she did the best she could for me all the time. Essie was a giver and a helper. Everyone in Latta, South Carolina knew that. My grandmother allowed other people to use our deep freezer. If people were homeless and she found out about it, they weren't homeless for long. She helped everybody.

Homeless persons that my grandma allowed to stay in our home would often stay in my sleeping quarters as my roommates. I never understood her logic of always helping needy people, especially because my room was shared with people I did not know. Sometimes I became angry why she had to help people she did not know. If they were hungry, she fed them; if they needed clothes, she clothed them; if they needed money and she had it, they got it, and the list goes on and on. She was an amazing human being whom I felt was often taken advantage of. She often said, "I didn't do it for them; I did it to please God. The indigent people whom she helped were merely just getting God's benefit. She always gave praise and Glory to her Creator.

When my grandmother felt I was old enough to work, I was sent to pick cucumbers in the hot sun. When I started, I was approximately seven years old. Every morning, bright and early, while still dark outside, white men would ride through our neighborhoods slowly, blowing their old ragged Ford 150 truck horns. Whoever wanted to work that day would come outside and jump on the back of the open bed trucks. When they had enough workers, they would drive straight to the cucumber fields, unloading their human cargo like sacks of potatoes and bales of hay.

I can still feel the damp air hitting my face as I held my hat and my rag on my head with my little hands. We all road together not looking at each other or saying a word. We were tired and sleepy. When we got off that truck, it was time to wake up and get to work. Some of my best advice and ideas came from brief conversations in the cucumber fields. I always tried to make the experience a positive one.

I went with these men who I didn't know to unfamiliar places to work in a vegetable field away from home.

Sometimes the ground would be so hot until, I would hide my bare feet under the cucumber vines, so they would stay cool. I labored hard, indefatigably. I picked as many cucumbers as I could every time, never slacking, never failing, always meeting the field foreman's daily goals.

Often, I picked cucumbers, laboring in three rows at one time. I wasn't afraid of snakes, insects, or worms back then. I had to work tirelessly — fear wasn't an option — fear could not help me pick cucumbers, only my efforts, my talents, only my work ethic could guide my path forward into the dirt fields lined with snaking vines and dust-layered vegetables. When we were done, the men backed their trucks against the field then drove around the entire field, surveying our accomplishments for a particular day. Then they hauled us away, along with our croaker sacks filled with cucumbers. After we were all on board, they took us to the gin yard to weigh and grade our cucumbers. My payroll checks were always between $6.00 to $7.00 per day, not bad for a child that wasn't even 10 years old yet. Because I was so young, they would cash the hand-written check for me.

Inside my grandparents' household, my early years were not difficult, yet they were demanding. My grandmother was a very devoted wife, mother, sister and friend. Although not affectionate, she was honest. She kept it real all the time. My grandmother cooked the meals, cleaned the house, washed clothes, and much more. She did it all. She was one hell of a woman. She taught me do the same. I had to learn to cook, clean, prime a pump, fetch water, chop wood, place coals in the stove, use a washboard to wash clothes, hang clothes on the line using clothespins, plant gardens, shell peas, ring a chicken's neck, and more were normal household duties for me, growing up in the South during those days.

I can still smell the scent of the chicken feathers from the times when we placed the chickens in the hot boiling water to soften their feathers, so we could pluck them. I fed the hogs slop, leftover food stored for days in buckets. Even though this was tough work, I was accustomed to doing it. As a result, I learned what hard times were while enjoying growing up in Latta. I don't regret my upbringing.

As I reflect on those times, I conflicted with many of my grandparents' southern traditions, strict-discipline and spirituality, which they had exposed me to. However, living with Grandma Essie was not easy; she created a set schedule of responsibilities and chores that I performed daily, unlike the way parents raise children today. For instance, as a young child, I woke up in the morning and performed household tasks immediately. First, I made up my bed then I washed my face, brushed my teeth, and put my clothes on before heading to the kitchen for breakfast. I could not get food from my grandmother's pots which sat on the stove, invitingly, hot and delicious to taste, or open her refrigerator door until I had washed and cleaned. And before I ate, I needed my grandma's permission to sit at the breakfast table. My grandmother wasn't a very affectionate person, but I knew she loved me.

The lack of affection was like a disease in my house. At times, I begged my grandmother for a hug or even a kiss on the cheek. When I would just hug her, she would always say stop with her hands close to her side. I'm sure this was what she had been exposed to as well. Maybe the emotional coldness was a southern way of life? I don't know, but I do know; I didn't like it at all. Therefore, that is why I kiss my children and grandchildren as often as I do now.

Although having a grandma who displayed little emotion or affection, her behavior influenced me to become more accepting of my own children by showing them tenderness. My emotional roller coaster was difficult, and it took years to do. I managed to turn it around! I hugged my children until it felt comfortable. I said, "I loved you until it no longer felt strange." I just changed over time. I was determined to get better. My immediate family is so affectionate now. It has truly become our way of life. Thinking back then, I believed affection wasn't normal. I learned to express my affection to my family and not believe it was abnormal. I was sick from the lack of it, and now I am determined to help others give it and receive it. The joy that love brings is so amazing.

My grandmother was not someone who wanted people to feel sorry for her. She was a humble servant. She was very active in church — Usher board, Eastern Star, Choir, etc…. She was also active in community and civic affairs in our town. Also, she was Latta's number one babysitter.

It would be several years later; November 1984, I lost my grandmother, Essie Bethea. My grandmother had heart failure at the age of 73 years old. She suffered for many years, silently, never complaining. Everybody knew Grandma Essie's health was getting worse, not improving. My grandmother said, "I never want to be a burden to anyone if I cannot do for myself, I'd rather just go home to meet my maker."

To receive better treatment and get properly diagnosed, she visited to New York City. While in NY, she had several strokes. These strokes left her paralyzed on both sides of her body.

I will never forget the day my grandmother came to the Latta High School where I was a student. To date, I still don't know her reason for coming to the school. That was out of the norm. She hardly ever visited any of the schools I was attending, unless she was cleaning them.

She was leaving for New York again for more treatments after she left the school. I knew that much. I remember how I felt watching from the window of my class, as my uncle slowly opened the back door for my grandmother. As she got in the back seat of the car, all I could see was the back of her head as she rode off in the car with my relatives. That image lives inside of memory even on today.

I asked my teacher to allow me to go and say good bye to my grandmother. I begged my teacher to "PLEASE LET ME SAY GOOD BYE TO MY GRANDMOTHER." Repeatedly, I asked, but my teacher, Mrs. Art refused.

That was the last time I saw my grandmother alive. I despised that teacher for years. I felt somewhere deep down inside me that would be the last time I would see my grandmother alive.

My feelings were correct.

A month or so later, I don't remember the exact month or date but, I have never forgotten the experience. It was a November afternoon, after lunch, strangers came to my Social Studies classroom. People, who I had never seen before, knocked on door and asked to see Tamia Sharonnette Bethea. They asked for me, but they didn't pronounce my name correctly. My teacher, Mr. Rice was trying to understand who they were asking for. Not too many people knew me by my first name. They all knew me by Sharonnette.

My feet felt heavy as I stood up and moved towards the strangers. That short walk felt like it was a mile long. At the time, I was 16 years of age in my 11th grade year, 1984. I made it to the door; a soft weakness came over my body. I knew then that their presence and news were not going to be good. The strangers and I ambled down the hallway to an unlocked room. A quietness settled over the room; through an open window, a slight breeze blew a sheet of paper from the teacher's desk onto the floor creating a ruffling sound.

I knew then, that it was my grandmother, the only person I had left that I knew really loved me, My Essie, my momma, was gone as quietly as the wind. She left me just like my mother and my grandfather did. Before the visitors could tell me, what had happened, I just said it. I told them my grandmother was dead. I said to them, "She's dead, right?" They confirmed my conjecture; I was correct. I don't remember much of anything after that. I had to be medicated. This was one death that I understood, and I took it with much difficulty. I was depressed and angry for a long time. I didn't understand why all of this was happening to me. It just didn't feel fair or right. That was one of the most difficult events I had to deal with in my life. However, following my grandmother's death, my life as I knew it was about to change forever.

It was time for me to grow up. Let the hard-times get harder. Boy did I mature through some stuff. I started to see everyone for who they really were. I learned that a lot of people who claimed to love me and care for me, were only pretending to satisfy my grandmother. I had to be strong and make adult decisions at 16 years of age.

It took me years to accomplish a long-time goal. I always wanted to become captain of the cheerleading squad. When my grandmother died, I was voted captain of the Varsity Cheerleading squad, and I had to resign to head north to live with other family members.

My grandmother had made a promise to me. She promised she would come and see me graduate, and she died before that happened. My grandmother never attended any of my extra school activities. She was either too tired, busy being who she was (an excellent mother, babysitter etc...), or just didn't want to be bothered. I remember the talent shows I entered, the softball team I made, the cheerleading squads I qualified for and not once did anyone from my family attend.

I felt alone most of my childhood. I felt that my accomplishments were mine and mine alone. They only mattered to me. It didn't matter how excited I became about situations or events in my life. I found dealing with death and its emotional pain were difficult to handle.

My grandmother or my grandfather didn't come ever. I saw other students with their parents. They spent family time together after the games. I walked home, often by myself, promising repeatedly that when I had children I would be active in their school affairs — often and as much as possible. I did, and I continue to do so even now.

I save all the programs from events I've attended with my children and grandchildren, especially those activities when they participated. I save notes that they wrote to me when they were younger, all the cards that I've gotten over the years and tons of pictures of us celebrating their success no matter how big or small. We often look at these keepsakes and laugh together as we remember the good times. The smiles on their faces are priceless. We continue to add to future memories.

Imagine dealing with all of this at 16 years old. I often felt like my life was just not worth living anymore. I felt like I really didn't matter. I felt like nobody cared about me or for me. I just didn't want to exist. I felt like no one would miss me because they didn't notice me anyway. I wanted the pain to go away. I was ready to end it all. I thought about suicide several times, too many times to remember!

My mind was playing games with me. Therefore, we must have people to talk to. People who get it. People who care about people. I was stuck in a bad place for a while. All these things happening to me before I turned 18. What was it about me? What was my problem? What did I do so bad to deserve this life? These questions often popped in my head.

I had no more time to waste. I had to get it together. I had to do it fast!

But, I am glad I overcame those early demands: family values, differing principles and philosophies. I became a better person because of my grandparents. I believe every child needs a touch of Grandma Essie and grandpa Earlie's upbringing.

I learned so much from my grandparents and have admired older people so much. I love to sit and listen to them. I feel like they have so much wisdom. Most of them just wanted to shower me with their life experiences. Older people were solution oriented. I listened to them all day.

My Father's Parents

I knew even less about my father's family. Don't get me wrong, my great grandmother Rose was good to me. She and her husband, my great grandfather, treated me like family. I learned how to shoot, chop wood, make homemade sausage, use a wood stove etc ....

On the other hand, my father's mother was very different. After discovering how she really felt about my mother, helped me to understand why she treated me the way she did. After all, I was my mother's child. I looked just like my mom. My grandmother, my father's mother, pretended to accept, love and cherish me when my father was present. Her energy in my father's absence translated into something different. I knew how she truly felt about me and my deceased mother deep down inside. As I always say, "Energy don't lie."

My grandmother struggled to raise me while my father's family was on the other side of town and didn't volunteer to help in anyway whatsoever. That's another reason I loved my grandmother Essie so much. She did the best she could with what she had. She never complained. She never asked anybody for anything. She never made me feel like I was a burden or a problem. She treated me as though she gave birth to me. She made due with what she had, and we came to understand that. She made me feel wanted.

In my present life, I have a couple of regrets. Specifically, I anguish because I did not tell my father's mother, Pleasant Mae, how I felt about the way she treated me and my children before she died. I felt neglected and disrespected when I was around her, very discouraging. Because of this, I kept my distance from her for years. My grandchildren felt it to and refused to allow her to hold them and in some instances, touch them. Once again, energy doesn't lie on people. You are who you are until you change!

I had very few regrets. One of them was not telling my father's mother how I felt about the way she treated me and my children before she died. No one wanted to feel neglected or disrespected. I felt like that every time I was around her.

"Although, my struggles were present in my earlier life, I was blessed with grandparents who I consider my Angels."

> "Yet at age seven, my innocence was overwhelming; the concept of death was very foreign, mystical, strange."

My Parents

My Mother, Sharon Bethea

ALTHOUGH MY MOTHER was around occasionally, my grandparents raised me. Because of this, I had a much stronger relationship with my grandparents than my mother, Sharon. My mother was the youngest of 11 children. She was the baby. I had an acceptable relationship with my mom. My mother was very young when I was born, and she often lacked patience with me.

She disciplined me sometimes for ridiculous reasons. I referred to her as "Sharon" and not mommy. She was more like a neighborhood friend or a big sister who bullied me around. I felt like we were not related some of the time because of her indifference to me. I honestly thought she hated me because of the way she treated me, causing me to fear her when she became angry because I didn't want to say the wrong thing. Unfortunately, it didn't matter because sometimes she would hit me because she thought I was going do something wrong. Whenever she was challenged by my grandparents for hitting me, she would say she did it because she thought I was going to do this or that. Can you imagine? Having to coup with her uneasy behavior at the tender age of to 7 years of age was not easy. I could not leave. I kept hoping life would get better for me.

She seldom smiled warmly, played affectionately, conversed openly, kissed or hugged me lovingly when I was a child. She whipped me for no reason — punishments that made little sense to me during this period. My grandparents often saved me from my mom's unprovoked drubbings. Sometimes when my mom would start to lambaste me, my grandparents stopped her, and other times she would already be flailing me, and they would intervene. Thank God for Essie and Earlie!

For instance, once my mother had cooked liver. Never had I eaten liver before. I asked her could I have some, and she said, "Are you sure you are gonna eat it?" I said, "Yes." When she gave it to me, I tasted it. I thought to myself, 'Oh! I am in trouble.' I hated the way it tasted. I sat there for a while. I didn't know what to do. I was so scared. When she noticed that I wasn't going to eat it, she gave me the worse beating that I had ever received from her. I fled under the bed to avoid the beating, but she lifted one end of the bed with one hand and beat me with the other hand.

Another time I received a whipping for which I did not understand occurred during dinner when I asked my mother for a second serving of fried chicken. Instantly, she became so angry that she gave me the entire bowl of chicken and sat me on the floor and forced me to eat it. When I couldn't eat all the chicken, my grandparents sat on the floor with me, and we ate the chicken together. I still bear the emotional scars from those episodes with my mother, and the pain and embarrassment haunted me for years, even today.

Whenever my mother went away to work in North Carolina, I was so happy. North Carolina had many tobacco fields. Handling tobacco was her trade. She was very fast and efficient. Just like her parents, she was a very talented and worked hard in the fields every day, picking and packing tobacco. My mom was paid well for handling tobacco; at least she thought so.

The amazing thing was when she came back home, she would always bring back some caramel nut candy for me, my favorite. I loved that candy. I can still taste the caramel melting in my mouth! I became excited when she said, "Guess what? I have something for you."

My mom loved me deep down inside, but I came to realize that she didn't know how to express it well. She was in a relationship that she didn't want to be in and had me, a child that came because of that relationship. She did the best she could, following examples from her parents who had shared little affection towards her as well.

Her affection was seldom shared with me. Possibly some of her lack of affection toward me evolved from her difficult childbirth with me. I heard the same story from different people. Maybe, they just wanted to make sure I knew. I was told that she was in labor with me for four days. I didn't know then but I understand now what that must have felt like for a teen mom. I mean that had to be a lot for a 17 year-old teenager. It was sort of like a baby having another baby.

Several years later, when I came of age, I experienced similar feelings. I to was in labor with my oldest daughter, Shavon for four days. I was 19 years old at the time. I felt then what my mother had experienced. Birthing my eldest child was one of the worse times of my life, but at the same time, Shavon's birth was one of the best times of my life.

Often, when my mother was angry with me, she would say, "I would die before I have another baby." She expressed those words quiet often. She used them so much that they came to life. I'm sure that if she knew how powerful her words were and how quickly they transferred into negative energy, she would have spoken different words. I had become very conscious of my thoughts and my words when I conversed with my own children. My mother's personal experience impacted my life immensely, influencing the way I speak and think today.

When I was about seven years old, my father and mother had separated by this time; he lived in New York, and my mother lived in Kingston, North Carolina with her boyfriend. My parents separated because they could not get along; they fought most of the time while they were together. My mother was a fighter, an angry person, landing in jail many nights for fighting. My grandparents always bailed her out of jail until my mother decided to leave our home and move to Kingston, North Carolina.

When I was about seven years old, my mother came back to Latta, South Carolina from North Carolina. The purpose of her brief visit was to tell our family about her health problem. She called me into the bathroom, first. As I entered, I found her sitting on the toilet. I can still see her face. She looked at me and told me she was going to die. I guess when she realized that I didn't quite understand, she wanted to help me comprehend by showing me.

While sitting on the toilet, she opened her legs and showed me what was in the toilet. It was a pool of blood — a toilet full of blood — blush-colored water staining the sides of the toilet.

I knew the blood had to come from her. I just didn't understand where the blood was coming from on her. I thought nothing would never happen to my mother because she was loud, bold, and tough, too. I associated her loudness with strength. I thought she was the strongest person in the world. I was having a tough time deciphering my mother's health problem. Why was this happening to her? What was going on really? I just didn't get it. My mom's health issue didn't make sense. After all, this was the first time I was hearing about death. Even though I had my own personal ideas about what death was at the time, I didn't know it meant her life would end permanently, and she would die and not return home. I didn't know; I wouldn't see her walking around, talking, screaming, etc....

I was seven years of age, still a baby to most, shocked and did not understand that my mother was ill, suffering from Ectopic — pregnancy in the Fallopian Tube. I didn't know anything about menstruating, pregnancy, sex, nothing. My grandmother and I never discussed sex or any topic involving human sexuality, even when I was old enough to understand.

My grandmother became incensed when she discovered my mother in the bathroom discussing her ailment with me. She told my mom to stop showing me blood and telling me she was going to die. She informed my mother that I was too young to understand. I was really confused. I didn't understand the reasons that inflamed my grandmother over this incident. As usual, I kept my mouth closed.

I just didn't understand; I wanted to know what was happening. I became even more curious. I thought about death intently after this episode. I asked my older cousins about my mother's illness when no one was listening. They supplied more confusing responses and just puzzled me even more. I needed to know exactly what was ailing my mother and no one gave me information that satisfied my curiosity or understanding of the situation that would be impacting my life soon. I was determined to uncover the truth.

Yet very young, my innocence was overwhelming; the concept of death was very foreign, mystical, strange. My grandmother often said, "One day you will understand it all better by and by." She was right. As I matured and grew older, I gained wisdom to understand my mother's condition.

She saw my interest and wanted me to really comprehend the plight she was facing. She simply didn't stop there, showing me the blood yet offering little explanation as to the nature of her sickness. Her actions were typical of how she handled problems, and how she communicated them to me.

After leaving the bathroom, she took me into my little bedroom where she kept her Bible, a large black leather King James Bible with gold-leaf pages. She fanned the pages looking for passages that she wanted me to read out loud to her. I did the best I could, but I didn't understand what I was reading. I knew it was the Bible, but the language didn't make since to me. She then started reading scriptures to me. Even though I didn't understand, it stirred up emotions in me, anxiety and despair. Those feelings remain today, reflecting on the moment as I contemplated my mother's sickness as I found it immutable, indelible on my mind.

My mother's boyfriend told her to stop reading scriptures. He became aggravated with her; I saw his frustration, creeping across his countenance.

He felt like it was a waste of time trying to get me to understand. I was simply too young to apprehend the enormity of it all. He felt she was scaring me and making me feel uneasy. He was correct. I did not understand.

To this day, I never understood what she had hoped to accomplish by showing me all the blood in the toilet and reading scriptures. I was messed up mentally. I didn't sleep well for days after that.

I dreamed about death for days at a time. I kept all those thoughts inside as I often did during that time period. I no longer wanted to strike up a conversation involving death, yet I was determined to figure this all out on my own for the peace of my little brain.

Reflecting on the situation with my mom, I believed that all of this was her way of showing me that she loved me. She was closing the chasm that for so long had separated us,

> "I dreamed about death for days at a time."

that had kept us from communicating, that had made us strangers in our own home.

Prior to her death, she touched me in a loving way, and she talked to me with a calm tone in her voice, no yelling or screaming, just affectionate conversations that I had sought for so long.

I started to feel comfortable with her. I started to like her at that moment. I believed she felt lovingly as me. Even though we were going to be separated for a long time, she would always be with me. My mother was really trying to make peace with me before she died. I felt like she knew death was knocking at her door, fast and furious. All she wanted and needed to do was to say sorry to me in the best way she knew — her own way.

My mother and I shared a lot of unpleasant moments together. She knew how unhappy she made me feel most of the time, and she realized that I was very afraid of her. In those last moments, we shared, I knew she loved me, cared about me in a motherly way for the first time in our lives.

After a short visit, she and her boyfriend returned to North Carolina. My cousin, Elliott, who lived with us at the time, was aware of my mother's behavior during her visit with us. I think she told him also. He was old enough to understand it all. Elliott was very close to my mother. He was the son of my late aunt Betty. My grandmother was raising us together when my mom became ill. Elliott and I were very close, and we still are today. After my mother left for North Carolina, I remember Elliott waking up every morning and saying, "Sharon is dead!"

My response was the same, "No, she was not dead."

Elliott knew I was afraid of the whole situation. I was aware that death was something to be sad about because of his reaction. When I think about it, maybe he was trying to prepare me for what he knew was going to happen. In just a few days, I think three to be exact, after my mom and her boyfriend returned to North Carolina, my grandmother received a phone call early one morning. My intuition kicked it, and before she answered the phone, I was certain what the call was going to be about. I had a strong feeling that day was the day she would hear that my mother had died.

I knew that this was the day Elliott would cry for real. Shortly after grandma Essie answered the phone, I heard a loud scream from her. This was a scream I had never heard before. I sat in the middle of my bed and didn't move, frozen. That was it; it was over; it had happened; it was finished; death had arrived and claimed my biological mother, Sharon. Elliott cried the loudest. I remained stoic, never shedding a tear.

I found difficulty displaying grief and emotional outbursts about my mom's death. I don't know how I really felt, confused and drained of affection that had escaped down a lonely dirt road in South Carolina.

During this time, no one ever told me that my mother had died or explained what happened. No one ever hugged me and told me that it was okay to shed a tear or discussed death with me. No one gave me permission to grieve. Numbness enthralled my being; I was confused again, unable to kiss and hug my grandparents.

It was like I was enveloped within a featured movie, in a theater watching myself play a role that I did not know the lines, a role that I had not prepared for, a role that was disheartening, sad, filled with pain and anxiety. After all, little girls were seen but not heard in those days.

I just went with the flow. I just dealt with my mother's death on my own the best way I knew how. It was strange hearing everybody talk about my mom's death and making funeral plans for her. I just listened and tried to make sense of it all. My grandmother had to make calls to my mother's sisters and brothers. She called my mother's friends, teachers, hanging out partners, and co-workers. She called the church and some of the members. I heard her tell the same story repeatedly until I started saying it in my mind. I knew which line was next during the conversation.

My mother had discussed her funeral arrangements with my grandmother; it was very clear what she wanted at her funeral. I knew she didn't want her body to be given to the local funeral home directors but instead to someone else. For some reason, she had major issues with the local funeral home director. Even my grandmother didn't understand that. Apparently, my mom had already organized all facets of her funeral. Everyone knew his or her own place.

I couldn't imagine, at the age of 24, planning my own funeral. I couldn't imagine knowing I was going to die then sharing that with all who would listen. My mother did. That had to be problematic for my grandmother. My mother was her last child, giving birth to my mom in the late 1940s. My mom was my grandma's "baby girl." My mother was her father's "baby girl" too. He loved Sharon and Tamia. I loved him to.

All of her sisters and brothers returned to south from New York and abroad to attend her funeral. We road to the church and to the graveyard in the limos. My ponytails and my bang looked so pretty as I walked around in my cute little white dress, not unlike the white dress my mom was wearing in the casket. She looked beautiful too, laying still and quiet in the casket. My grandmother believed in doing things first class, and she loved being original. Essie wanted the best for us all even in death.

I still hold that image in my head today. I remember the special vault that she was laid to rest in. As a matter of fact, it is still in decent shape after forty plus years.

My feelings were conflicted; I loved my mom, but on the other hand, I just wanted her to stop yelling and beating me. I wanted the abuses to disappear, not my mom. I wanted peace and quiet for once in my young life. While my mom laid in the vault, I whispered to myself, "She can't beat me anymore."

Thank GOD! What a way for a young girl to think about her mother. All the beatings that I had gotten from my mother started to replay in my mind like reruns at the movie theater. The more I looked at my mom in that steel vault; the angrier and happier I became. I knew that the painful part of my life was over. I was thankful for that at least for the moment.

During the funeral, I heard my cousin, Jerry, my mother's best friend and hanging out buddy, scream. Jerry and my mother were like two peas in a pod. For me, tears never came to my eyes during the funeral or at the burial. I was busy taking my mom's death scene all in, watching the events unfold, watching her relatives cry and scream while I sat stoic and immutable to it all; my heart froze like my emotions, cold and stiff.

I remember several people telling me that I had encouraged them on that day by the words that I spoke. Even today, I can't remember who I talked to and or what I said. However, I have shed many tears after her death. Although, my mother treated me badly, I needed her in my life.

Today, I sincerely realized that my mother did the best she could base upon what she knew or what she thought was right.

Babies don't come with "THIS IS HOW TO RAISE YOUR CHILD" manuals. As parents, we had to figure it out as we ventured along understanding that each child was different, and using child-rearing practices like those which we experienced as children.

To avoid raising my children in the manner which I was raised, I had to free myself of those negative emotions and preconceptions that were forced on me years ago. What a blessing to forgive and let go. I was healed because of this. I felt like weights were lifted off my shoulders. My transformation didn't happen overnight. It took a lot of workshops, a lot of teachers, a lot of energy, a lot of counselors, a lot of money, but it was worth it as I watched my children grow and mature as I did with them — growing and maturing.

Eventually, I discovered how my mom died. She was pregnant in her tubes (ectopic pregnancy). Her fallopian tube erupted while she was asleep and the blood filled her stomach, and some blood travelled to her brain. She died instantly.

Because I knew her bleeding started long before her tube erupted, I often wondered why she didn't seek medical attention. For all I know, she could have gone to the doctor and nothing was done, or maybe she simply refused service.

I don't know, and I may never know. From what I understand, her boyfriend was very crest fallen, lugubrious over her death. I wish I knew where he was today. I am sure he could answer a lot of questions for me. Who knows, maybe he will read this book and we will reconnect. He was an amazing kind man. He made my mother happy and I could see it even through her pain.

Even though I traveled this road, if I had the opportunity to redesign my life, I would choose this kind of upbringing less the beatings.

I started losing people early on in my life. This is one experience I will never forget. I had a very close childhood friend named Lizzie Ann. Boy, we were so close. She was such a beautiful perfect human being. She never judged me. We never argued. She just loved me, and I loved her to. She had a tire swing in her backyard that we often played on. One day, she played on the tire swing by herself. Her mother called her several times to come in and help wash the dishes, but Lizzie Ann never answered. When her mother got tired of calling her, she went outside to look for her. She found Lizzie Ann. Lizzie had gotten her neck tangled up in the rope that was holding the tire from the tree. She had accidentally strangled herself.

This was another time in my life I felt responsible for being too close to someone. I thought maybe if I had not befriended her she would have never died.

I was beginning to believe that everybody I loved too much, too long or too hard would die or go away. I was beginning to think it was not safe to get close to people or allow people to get close to me. I started distancing myself from people. Many people thought I was stuck up, rude, mean, and even some felt I was arrogant and downright disrespectful. It wasn't that at all. How could I be some of or even all those things with little of nothing. To them, I assumed, it didn't matter. All I know is I thought I was protecting them and they didn't even know it! I felt they would someday appreciate it.

What most people didn't see was the invisible self-inflicted mental abuse I was caring around for years. What they didn't see was those invisible wounds that had not healed yet. I was a hurting toddler and teenager. I was making myself sick. I held a lot inside. I thought I was suppose to. I later understood what it was. My past experiences were the real reasons why I was behaving the way I did. I thought by not allowing people into my personal circle, I was helping them. I was protecting them, keeping them safe from me. I didn't want them to die like all the others. For a very long time, I would not allow people to get close to me. I would not get close to others. When I noticed I was letting my guard down, I would quickly build a wall. I stayed to myself on purpose feeling like I was doing a good thing. I was protecting the world from me. I was a loner for a long time.

My Father, Willie Bethea

During my earlier years, I did not spend much time with my father, Willie Bethea, who was often absent from the home, fought vigorously with my mom. My dad and mom had separated very early in their marriage. I have a few very vague memories of my father when I was growing up. I really didn't know him on a personal level. I just knew he existed.

I was nine years old when he was arrested. I heard family members talking about him and what they thought he had done. I say thought because my father has always told me, he didn't do it. I never judged him. This was between him and GOD, the ultimate judge. I heard, at the age of 9 years old, my father received a double life sentence and would never see the light of day. To me double life meant, I would never see my father again.

For me, this was not something that I initiated in conversation. As a matter of fact, it was off limits when it came into discussion. I was protecting myself from being judged. I never talked about my father's incarceration with others because I thought they would think I was just like my father. I thought they would have misjudged me because my father was a convicted felon.

I was fortunate to have a grandmother like mine. She played a huge part in keeping my dad and I connected. She knew how I felt about him, the situation, the disappointment. She didn't talk about it around me much either. It was just a conversation that was often avoided. Even though, we struggled to eke out a living and ongoing challenges with finances, my grandmother, still accepted collect calls from my father. She never refused any of his calls. She let me talk to my father whenever he called. I never lost contact, never.

My father wrote to me often. He never forgot my birthday, special holidays, etc... Even when I became a mother, he sent his grandchildren birthday cards, card for special holidays etc .... He was selfless back then.

He thought of us often. Even though he wasn't there to attend any of my graduations, high school, college, or very special occasions, he always made me feel like he was proud of me. I could feel his love in the cards, letters he sent to me and my children. He may not have gone with me to the Justice of Peace to witness my first marriage, or come to the hospital when I gave birth to his first grandchild, he may not have been there when his first grandson and second granddaughter came into the world, he may not have been there when I was growing through so much "stuff," he kept in touch.

I was 33 years old when my father was released from prison after being locked up for 25 years of his life. He and I bonded as though we were never separated.

I loved my father. It wasn't until, my father was incarcerated in New York when I was older that I really got the chance to communicate and open the dialogue door with him. I remember visiting him in jail for the first time. I was already all married with 2 small children. As I prepared to see my father, I often thought about the way I would react. All that I thought about went out the window when I saw him.

Sometimes I would say I would do this or that, say this or that, and when the time came to respond, I did it completely different. That was me. I knew I had lots of questions to ask him. I was hoping I could get answers to gain closure. I wanted to know why he didn't come to my mother's funeral. I wanted to know why he went to prison and left me to be raised by my mother's parents. I wanted to know why his mother, his brothers and sisters acted like I never existed most of the time.

The day I went to the prison to visit my father was one of the most exciting yet nerve raking days ever. I remember that visit very well. I sat there in the waiting room while the officers went to get him. Every time the door opened, I would look and see if it was my dad. I had not seen him since I was around 8 years old. I sort of remembered what he looked like. I didn't know what to expect but I knew that I would know him when I saw him.

When the door opened, I saw my father walk through the iron doors; I knew it was him, even though he had changed as he had gotten older. When I saw my father come through that door, all I could do was quickly walk over to him as fast as I could and hug him. The tears flowed from both our eyes like streams upon the cold tiled prison floor. We hugged a very long time, years passed through our arms during that moment.

> "The tears flowed from both our eyes like streams upon the cold tiled prison floor."

We cried together. I felt like a little girl all over again. My father knew I would want to know about his circumstances, and he was prepared to answer all my questions. As a matter of fact, he asked me to ask him anything. I asked every question; I could think of. He responded to them all. My questions were answered as far as I was concerned. I left there feeling like I had just put another piece of my life puzzle in its place.

He told me that he wasn't at the funeral because he was in New York City at the time, and by the time he found out about my mom's death she had been buried. Also, he said he heard my mother had an enlarged heart and that's what killed her. I told him the truth.

He explained why he went to prison. He said he didn't commit the murders that he was accused of. He said he took the blame for somebody else. He said the person who did it had children and was pregnant with another child. He felt sorry for her and didn't want her to go to jail and lose her children etc…. He said he felt that if my grandmother, his mother, got a lawyer, he would have been freed immediately. Nonetheless, his mother never got a lawyer as she promised she would, and he spent 25 years in prison.

Instead of getting a lawyer, she took out an insurance policy. I think she didn't expect him to leave there alive. She was wrong. Little did she know, she would expire before he would. May God bless her soul.

Imagine spending 25 years in jail for something someone else had done. I couldn't imagine that. Unfortunately, there are a lot of people in jail for something he or she didn't do. I pray for them all. I also believe that everything happens for a reason. Had my father not gone to prison when he did, he may not have been here to tell the story. According to him, he was on the fast train to destruction. Jail slowed him down. He became a man and now makes better decisions because of it. I am not promoting jail in no way. What I am saying is that for him, it could have been a matter of life or death on the streets of New York.

On a positive note, my father was a free man when his two great grandsons, Jaylen and Jeremy were born. He attended my graduation celebration when I got my cosmetologist license. We have had some great moments, and we continue to do so. My father was also around when I met and fell in love with my soulmate, Anthony Phillip Williams Sr.

My father was like my right-hand man. He was the best grandfather and great grandfather any child could ask for. He was a friend, a social worker, a policeman, a preacher, a lawyer, a judge, doctor, mentor, motivational speaker, an encourager, comforter, and more all wrapped up in one big daddy package.

We all talk to my father in confidence and never have to worry about it getting out. I admire him for that. He's someone that can be trusted. He's a man with very few words and integrity comes naturally to him. My daughters and my son have attested to that. They simply adore him. My mother would have been proud to say that was her husband. Whenever we needed him, he made our business his business. Always, he found ways to help us to achieve anything we wanted. I knew my father loved my mother, and he still does.

He cries when he talks about her. Certain love songs that he hears make him cry over her as well. They loved each other. They were just young and immature. It just didn't work out for them. However, I felt very blessed to have had a relationship with both of my parents no matter what the situation or circumstances were. They were very different relationships, and I learned from them both. These relationships have helped me grow, mature, and change areas of my life that needed attention.

"Although, my struggles continued in my earlier life, I was blessed with parents who I consider my Angels."

Leaving the South

The Train Ride North

BEFORE MY GRANDMOTHER left to go to NY, she left me with a family in Latta, SC. My grandmother babysat for this family for years. In the beginning, it was nice. I was consoled and encouraged; everyone appeared concerned about what I had gone through in 16 short years.

This was short lived. It's mind boggling how people act like they or shall I say pretend like they love someone so much when others are watching them love on someone and how they quickly stop loving that person when people are not watching. This was my experience most of my life especially after my grandmother died. It was like I became a light switch, turning love off and on as desired.

I felt surrounded by hypocrites all the time. I stayed in a very uncomfortable environment, feeling like a stranger in somebody else's home. I didn't feel welcomed at all. At times, I was hungry and stayed hungry after breakfast and dinner because I was afraid to ask for more in fear of rejection. I didn't want to bring embarrassment to myself or shame to my past.

This new situation, living with my grandma's employers, was a much different life than the one I had with my grandparents. Previously, I could eat until I was full or until the prepared meal was gone, whichever one came first. I could go in the refrigerator and get a drink if I was thirsty. Home was like home for me growing up with my grandparents. My family walked to church together every Sunday. This new situation was very different. I rode in the back seat with the husband while the other children, all girls, either rode with their mother or drove themselves in their cars. It was not an easy pill to swallow. They would go out to eat after church while I would ride in the back seat of their father's car back home. I stayed in the shared bedroom most of the time. I felt like I was a burden. I felt like I was not welcomed in their home at all. Little did I know this was just the beginning. It got worse as I moved on and got older. My grandmother would say, "You will miss me when I'm gone." I didn't understand that until she was gone. I often thought about those words. I did understand it all better as time progressed.

Like any other 16 year-old teenager, I started to act out. I was angry, tired of being mistreated. I wanted OUT! I felt like they didn't like me and started to slowly explode. I developed an "I don't care attitude." When I finally got their attention, it wasn't the kind I was looking for; however, the next thing I knew I was on my way to Dillion, South Carolina to catch the Amtrak train with a one-way ticket to New York along with a very profound message. I didn't know who I was going to be staying with. I knew nothing. I was afraid of New York life. All I heard was negative things about New York since I could remember. No one in South Carolina had anything good to say about New Yorkers. We often referred to them as city slickers, yankees, and fast talkers. What a bunch of stereotypes!

The woman who my grandmother left me with, drove me to the train station. It was just the two of us. It was the coldest darkest ride ever. We didn't speak the entire ride. Although this was normal behavior, it felt weird this time. As we arrived at the train station, she said, "Here is $50.00." She told me to go to New York and make something of myself. She told me not to become a prostitute or start selling or using drugs. I never forgot the tone in her voice. She drove off. She had gotten rid of her problem, me. No handshake, no hug, no positive words, no smile, and no kiss. I thought this time I would be shown a little love or affection, but I was super wrong. The tears fell down my face as I left her sight. I felt hated. I felt disliked. I felt like a failure. I felt useless. I felt alone again! I was on my own. I didn't have a clue as to what to do next. I thought to myself "Tamia NOW what!"

At that time, the train ride to New York was the longest ride I had ever taken by myself. For the first time in my life, I was afraid, afraid of the journey, afraid of where I was headed, afraid of who I would meet and even who I would become.

I had much to think about. Little did I know there was more where that came from. All I could say to myself was wow. I didn't know grown people behaved that way. My grandmother left me in their care because she trusted I would be treated fairly and cared for the way she cared for their children and cared for me. She chose who I stayed with very carefully. She was basing it off what personality she saw when they were around she and me together. In her presence I was treated like royalty. In her absence, well you know. This in your face personality was the only thing my grandmother had nothing else to go on.

Talk about being bitter, I was very upset with my grandmother, the woman that I looked at as being my real mother. I was upset with her for leaving me in such a mess. I wanted to just die. I was emotionally sick and becoming physically sick. I would wake up in vomit. I would try to make it to the bathroom to throw up and sometimes I didn't. Stress can become ones biggest baddest nightmares. It was becoming a part of me. I didn't like it.

I discovered that people transform to fool others. The real them shows up eventually. They can't hide forever. This happened to me several times.

All I was growing through appeared to be a box filled with disappointments and setbacks. I later realized I was being set up for great things. These disappointments and setbacks were really building blocks for success. I was enjoying my pity party so much until I didn't have time to appreciate my trials and tribulations. I didn't have time to notice the blessing in the test!

I had no idea at the time that all that I was growing through appeared to be a setback, but it was a setup for success. I was being set up for wonderful things. I was enjoying my pity party so much until I didn't have time to appreciate my trials and tribulations. They were all blessing in disguise.

Many times, I wanted to end my life. I wanted to make everybody happen by disappearing. I often thought of ways to commit suicide. Yes, those thoughts crossed my mind more than I care to remember. I was lonely, sad, depressed and simply put, very lost. Growing up I just felt that the pain was too much to bare. I felt like I was all alone in a big world of fake selfish people. I felt like I was being punished for something. I started blaming my mother, father, grandmother and grandfather for leaving me behind to deal with all of what I was dealing with by myself. I started questioning God. I was just angry.

I was always told it was more than one side to every story, but that only applied to the grownups. As a young lady, I never got a chance to share my side of the story until later in life. I always knew if I lived long enough that one day I would eventually tell my story. Now, I'm telling my story.

New York

When I arrived at Penn Station, I was picked up by my uncle and my cousin. As I entered the car, I felt tense; the negative energy was almost unbearable. Because the car was so small, I just held my suitcase in my lap and kept my mouth closed. I was afraid to talk.

I didn't know what was told to them. I felt like no matter what I would say It would be wrong anyway. I felt I had no wins in the situation period. I sat there with my suitcase thinking about my life as it was at that time. I came face to face with my own reality: I had to survive, no matter what. A mustard seed of desire and determination was planted in me at that very moment. I was ready for whatever!

My uncle and cousin never asked about my long ride on the train from the south to New York, nor did they mention anything about my reason for leaving Latta, nor did they ask about the people I lived with in Latta who stuffed all of my belongings into one old soiled clothing bag, like trash and who had sent me on my way to a strange land called New York, like a vagabond, an abandoned homeless gypsy, abandoned from my birthplace, abandoned from a life I knew growing up in the south.

Prior to my mother's parents' deaths, my great grandparents on my father's side were the best to me. They predeceased my grandmother. So, who was left? In my mind, nobody who wanted me was left.

My father's family was in the South, but they didn't want me; they never contributed to my livelihood; they never participated in my experiences. I was surrounded by people who I did not know, yet I was in the North, in an unfamiliar place, a great metropolis, an asphalt beast filled with terror and contempt that would surly devour me or forsaken me within my own jungle of fears and apprehensions.

This was not a joke nor dream, a nightmare that was really happening. All the feelings that were running through me were making me weak. I felt like no one cared about me in the same manner as my grandmother. It was an act: I had my beliefs, my strengths, my bundle of clothes, stuffed in a sullied laundry bag.

I left behind all my personal accouterments that I had accumulated through the years of growing up with my grandmother. Something was terribly wrong, no welcoming party, no parade or cheers, just coldness and a sense of loneliness encapsulated my mind.

I decided to go with the flow. First, I went to my aunt's house, my mother's birth sister. I knew she never wanted me there. We never bonded. When she saw me, she voiced little interest in knowing me or my situation or my past.

> "Something was terribly wrong, no welcoming party, no parade or cheers, just coldness and a sense of loneliness encapsulated my mind."

She told me to sleep on the couch. I was destined to live out of my suitcase during that period. There were beds there. She had a room so did my cousin, but me, I had the couch. I mean after all, who was I anyway that's how I felt.

My aunt and I never had a full amicable conversation. She didn't want to be bothered by her recent interruption, her burden from the South. I didn't want to be there, my recent interruption, my burden from the North. Our disdain for each other was mutual, unresolvable, uncompromising, unswayable. When she did communicate, she would jaw, "Are you going to eat it all?" Or, if I opened the refrigerator, she would query, "What are you looking for?" I seldom answered; I would shut the door and walk away.

Living with my aunt, she never provided a positive environment. I longed to disremember those moments there, but her negativism stuck like gorilla glue to my mind. I wish I could forget; trust me, I tried.

The day came, and I finally left and moved in with my uncle's wife, their daughter and a cousin in Queens, New York. Living with my uncle, his wife, and 2 cousins was a very interesting situation also. I was excited about leaving my other aunt. I felt good about being able to sleep in a bed and possibly getting to know my girl cousins.

My hopes of that were washed away fast. Quickly, my hopes were doused when I had to sleep in my new bedroom — a doorless cold space on the front porch. I slept in the day room downstairs by myself while everyone else slept upstairs.

It was always cold in that day room. So eventually, they gave me small heater to keep me warm. I thought that was nice. I did the best I could to keep warm.

In addition to the space heater, I kept warm with my grandmother's handmade blanket which she had sewn from my grandfather's old work clothes when I had lived at 208 Henry Street, Latta, SC. Not only did it keep me warm, from head-to-toe, it offered me symbolic protection. When I used that blanket, I felt like I was wrapped up with Essie and Earlie.

I hardly ever went upstairs. Downstairs where I was staying, there was a small bathroom, barley large enough for one person. I used that bathroom to wipe off, brush my teeth, and use the toilet. The other bathroom seemed to be occupied most of the time.

My aunt was kind; she had a welder to weld bars on the windows for my protection; however, I was ready for anything at this point. I just wanted time to pass, so I could move on with my life.

Springfield Gardens High School

In 1985, I will never forget my senior year when I enrolled at Springfield Gardens High School. My one year there left an indelible impression on my mind. Initially, the students at Springfield Gardens High and I didn't gel. They looked at me as strange. I was shocked when I heard students disrespecting teachers and doing things contrary to school rules. I often defended the teacher and chastised the students. Because I was viewed as being "different" or "old soul," a lot of my initial friends were from the South and many from Africa, the islands of Jamaica, Haiti, Trinidad, Granada and Guyana. They all had similar upbringing as me, no nonsense! Later in the year, my friend base grew. I never had to change who I was to fit in; people just gravitated towards me. I am still friends with many of them today.

At Springfield Gardens High School, I learned early on that I could begin to gain some sense of direction and satisfaction in my life. I spent hours in school. I would do anything to keep from going to the place I called home. I joined every school club I could squeeze into a school day and beyond. I tried out for cheerleading and made the squad. My little girl smile started to return.

In the beginning, I knew no one, and nobody knew me. I was a stranger in the middle of thousands of students, unlike the time when I spent at my former high school in Latta, South Carolina. I felt robbed of the opportunity to graduate with my friends in Latta. I had attended school with my classmates in the South from kindergarten to the 11th grade. We had history together; we were spanked together. We travelled on trips together. We were family. I missed them so much and thought of them all often.

In that same year, I got a job at a bank not far from where I lived and attended school. Working as a clerk at the bank became another psychological outlet for me. At the depository, I smiled more often than usual. The workers at the bank treated me like I mattered. Life was progressing well for me now. I was finding external extended families everywhere.

I adjusted to my new high school quickly. All my teachers knew I wasn't a New Yorker. They heard it in my speech; they saw it in my dress. My grandmother raised me well. I wore slacks and dresses while others wore jeans and sweats. I didn't have clothes like that. When I started working, I started buying a few leisure clothes every now and then. I tried to fit in without changing me; a viewpoint I still hold dearly today.

In my senior year in Springfield Gardens High School, I decided to make the best of it, have fun, participate in extracurricular activities, and have friends. Many of my peers treated me well also. I was accepted by most. They listened to me. My classmates wanted to hear my ideas and get my opinion. For once in my life, I felt wanted, accepted, and needed.

In the spring of 1986, my senior year was coming to an end: senior trip, prom, and graduation were near. I went to the Poconos on my Senior trip. On that outing, I met my children's future father. Because the school was so big, I never saw him during the school year. It took a school trip for us to meet.

Getting to know each other turned into a boyfriend girl-friend relationship. We went to the prom together. We were dressed so nice. I looked like a southern bell in my powder blue ballroom dress with long lace gloves and a matching powder blue lace trimmed umbrella. He looked like a southern gentleman in his powder blue tuxedo. We became Mr. and Miss Prom King and Queen that night. It was a prom to remember. We danced to "Always and Forever." It was awkward. But it was fun.

The principal even mentioned us in his speech at our graduation. I still remember the laughs and smiles that came from that. I felt so special. I hadn't felt that way in a while. Imagine your name being mentioned in front of a few thousand graduating students and parents. Someone of authority knew me and acknowledged that he did. Thank you.

College

Well it was time to go away to college. College was never something that I really wanted to do. I always had a business mind. I always knew I could do better for myself if I worked for myself. I didn't want to have to pay college tuition. I didn't want to owe anybody anything! I never saw my grandmother borrow any money from anybody. People were always borrowing from her. Borrowing wasn't a habit that I cared to form.

I was fortunate to have found out about a program that I could participate in. It was called the HEOP Program. Higher Education Opportunity Program for students who came with baggage pretty much. At least that's how I looked at it. Because my mother was dead, and my father was incarcerated, I automatically qualified for this program. I was accepted right away. I leaped on the opportunity especially after they explained the program to me. We had to go to the summer program and take a several preliminary preparation classes.

I was excited to be away from home. Long Island University, Southhampton Campus, I could hardly wait. I wasn't looking for a college degree; I was looking for privacy and solace, a place to relax, a bedroom, a living room — a home. This was my chance, and I took it. The degree was just a luxury, an incentive that I had not planned into my life prior to living in New York.

My uncle drove me to Long Island University to the Southhampton Campus for my orientation. That was one of the best days of my life. He seemed to be happy for me to. He and I talked the entire way there. He was a different person away from home. He appeared more relaxed, calm, and collected. It was a very nice ride.

College transformed my life. I started to put me back together again during my college years. I was smiling more, feeling happy, and energetic. I wanted to live again.

Little did I know that my emotional pain would resurface in my life. My children's father and I dated for 3 years before he asked me to marry him. I was 16 when we started dating. I was a sophomore in college, and he was in the military at the time of our engagement.

I remember my first semester in college prior to more of my unknown drama. It was an exciting time for me. I was already dating a young man whom I met my senior year in high school. I thought I had arrived. He had decided to go into the military, so he could make something of himself. I was okay with that. I thought it was a great idea. I had been around military men all my life. It was like almost all the men in my family had been into the US Army.

"Although, my struggles continued when I moved from South Carolina to New York and faced disappointments with my aunt and uncle, I was blessed with friends and teachers who I consider my Angels."

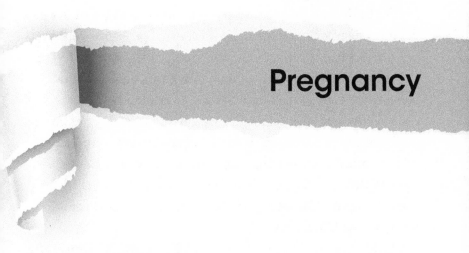

> "I emulated my mother's lack of affection and her indescribable scorn with my first daughter, Shavon."

Pregnancy

Family Disappointment

WHEN MY BOYFRIEND came home on leave to visit, he gave me an engagement ring, I got pregnant. We must have been overly excited that night because I got pregnant on the night we got engaged. Oh boy. Now what was I going to do.

I was in my second year of college, about to begin my Junior year of college when I became pregnant. Although I wasn't degree motivated, I didn't want to give one of my non-supporters something to talk about. Now I had to finish what I started. I remembered what my grandmother went through while babysitting children. I knew it wasn't an easy job. I automatically understood the importance of finishing school before the baby came.

I decided to get my degree as quick as possible. I found out that I could get it a year earlier if I were willing to work harder than ever. I was on a mission. I knew that If I didn't get it my degree before the baby was born, I probably would not finish. I had to do it. Going to several colleges and working several jobs wasn't easy. I had to get this done and that was my focus. It's amazing what we, as human beings, can do when we get laser focused. I was just that!

To expedite my college credits and graduation, I enrolled in two more colleges that were offering what I needed to complete my degree. Simultaneously, I attended LIU Southhampton Campus, Suffolk Community College, and Stony Brook University.

I did this for what purpose. I had to prove a point. I had to let everyone know I was not a failure. I was going to show the doubters that I could finish what I started. To me failure wasn't an option. I knew I was expected to fail, and I refused to allow anyone to dance to that tune.

My nerves were so bad. Reality was looking me in my face. Many conflicting thoughts jettisoned through my young mind. I had to decide. I knew I was going have my baby no matter what. I just had to figure out how I was going to accomplish so much so quickly. I wondered how I was going to keep this on the down-low, a secret, without anyone finding out. That didn't last for long. People discovered my pregnancy quickly. It was like they could smell the baby or something. My fiancé's family was excited. To them, family was as simple as adding another tablespoon of rice to the pot. This was no time for secret holding; they wanted the world to know. They started planning baby showers and all.

My life was in a tail-spin; I felt like the world knew too soon that I was pregnant. It was like someone had stood in the heavens with an earthly microphone and told everyone on the planet about my pregnancy. Because it didn't take long for the news of my pregnancy to spread, my good news became sad news. I was made to feel like crap because of a gift of life that was given to me to bring into the world.

I was getting funny looks, especially at church, in college, at home, seemed like everywhere. Everyone had an opinion about my pregnancy. Nobody asked me what I thought. I think this was the beginning of me developing a stronger attitude — "I don't care what you think of me predilection."

As far as my pregnancy, a few of my professors told me to stop coming to class because I was over pregnant, and it was making them nervous. They didn't want me to have the baby in their classes. The way I was going, they had a point. I would have probably gone into labor.

To say I was gigantic was an understatement! My stomach swelled immensely; I could hardly drive my car; my stomach touched my steering wheel, causing me some rather anxious moments.

However, my professors became some of my greatest supporters towards the end of my pregnancy.

Because of their faith in me, I could complete the balance of my assignments home.

When I wanted it bad enough, the stars just line up like soldiers in the army. Just know, I was on a mission of getting it done.

My family was a bit disappointed as I stated earlier. It was obvious. I could tell by the way they treated me and by the things I heard them say. I found out how they felt; they eventually exposed themselves. Many were negative about the pregnancy, period. Some family thought I had ruined my life.

One of my relatives said, "I know she would be nothing. She is going to fail."

Others said, "I told you she wasn't gonna be nothing."

More relatives said, "She done messed up her life. She will never finish school with a baby." Those words sat a fire in me that still burns today. I have been on fire for my life ever since. I never forgot those words. Those words helped me to just move ahead and break-neck speed to achieve. I had to win for me and my baby. Those words motivated the hell out of me. I was determined to shut their mouths by succeeding. Success became my friend!

I remember going to a doctor who my uncle recommended. That doctor tried everything he could to get me to have an abortion. It was like someone put him up to it. I was so pissed. I left out of his office knowing that I was pregnant, and my baby would be born on April 16, 1989. The doctor gave me a paper with several locations where I could go to terminate my pregnancy.

> "That doctor tried everything he could to get me to have an abortion."

It just wasn't me to do that, and I didn't. To me, it was just wrong to terminate — to do something that I felt so deeply against. To me, life was a blessing from my Creator, Jehovah; if I didn't give it, how could I take it away? Who was I to make that decision was how I felt. I asked God to have His way.

If it was meant to be great, if not that was ok to, I was staying out of it. I left that doctor's office knowing my baby would soon arrive if all went well because I was determined to keep my baby.

At the same time, I was saving my money and buying whatever I thought my baby would need. Because of my dedication and effort to accomplish my goals at that time, people that I hardly knew reached out and just started helping me. They saw I was determined and serious. I was consistent. I didn't have much of anything. I wasn't concerned about me, I was concerned about this little person that would soon be arriving. My friends and relatives gave three baby showers. I had so much stuff for my baby until it was mind blowing. I hardly had any room to store the baby's gifts. My baby wouldn't need anything for a long while.

During this time, I was in serious need of transportation. I went to the dealership and tried to get a car on my own. Because I didn't have any credit at the time, I was told I needed a co-signer. I asked my uncle. I was fortunate to have him agree to co-sign for me. Excitement came when I received the news of the loan being approved.

I was scheduled to pick the car up the next day. Upon arriving at the dealership, the following day, I was greeted by the dealer with terrible news. My uncle, who had already co-signed, changed his mind. I asked the dealer if he knew why. He began to share with me all the negative things my uncle told him about me, my fiancé and my unborn child.

He told me the reason why my uncle changed his mind was because I didn't have an abortion. I was in ultimate shock. Why? Who? Was I that bad of a person? The automobile dealer said he was told that I had a man and let him take care of it and me. When I heard this, it made me even more determined to work harder and faster to achieve my goals. I wanted independence and success in life, both from a personal and professional stand point.

When I have a burning desire, I believe there is always a ram in the bush. When nana, my children's father's grandmother, saw how determined I was to finish college, she was inspired to help me. She rented me a car for an entire week. This allowed me to attend three different colleges at the same time, which later allowed me to graduate, with a bachelors' degree, a year early. My daughter's father's aunt volunteered to co-sign for me to get a brand-new car. She did something for me that she hadn't done for anyone else including her own children. I will never forget the love that she showed me. She helped me to become the person I am today. She gave me a chance.

God was on my side, and I was feeling the love. I knew it then, and I really know it now. He was not holding back anything. I felt super blessed throughout my trials and tribulations. I learned to enjoy and most of all trust my trials and tribulations. I continued to experience victory at the end. Victory never failed me. Now when I see a trial or a tribulation, I know victory is near.

I refused to quit. Winning was my only option. I had such a burning desire that it was mind blowing. People started saying everything I touched turned to gold. Determination made me to act and that is what I did.

Shavon — My First Born

The time came to have my baby. I must have gone to the hospital 4 or 5 times prior to giving birth — false alarms. The physicians kept checking me and sending me home. I was so tired of hearing, its not time yet or you haven't begun to dilate. This went on for 4 full days.

I had a very good midwife. She was awesome. We had a plan. I wasn't gonna take any medication. I was gonna have my baby natural. I was gonna take the pain like a woman. After all, it couldn't be that bad. Please! Our plan went out the window. I thought I was going to die. It was the kind of pain that can't be explained.

During my entire pregnancy, I did not communicate with my boyfriend's mother. When she found out I was in the hospital, for some reason, she thought it was okay to just show up. This made me very uncomfortable. I knew I was not one of her favorite people, so I wasn't clear as to why she would want to be there. Why would she want to be around me. I wanted this to be a happy time within a happy environment for myself and our immediate family. Her presence made me anxious. I was hoping she would leave.

That was one of those times I wished my mother or my grandmother was alive. I would have been fine if my father was out of prison, also. Nevertheless, I was pregnant and in labor. Towards the end of the labor, I really didn't care who was in the room, at least that's how I felt. I didn't care who saw or didn't see whatever. All I wanted was for that baby to exit my body. I wanted my baby to come out not then but yesterday. I was in pain!

My wish came true. My midwife and future mother-n-law were not getting along in the delivery room. My midwife had the answers because she was there with me throughout my entire pregnancy. She knew me. My boyfriend's mother thought she had all the answers because she was the mother to many children. Because they were not cooperating with the doctor and nurses, they were put out of the delivery room. I wanted my midwife to be there but having my daughter's father there was enough support. After all what could I do besides pray and push.

Eventually, the doctors broke my water and induced my labor. I thought that was a good thing. I said to myself, "I am so glad I have a smart doctor. He is helping me by inducing my labor. That was so sweet." I didn't really understand what that meant. I discovered soon enough: the pain was unbearable.

Finally, it was time to leave that room. I had dilated the full 10 centimeters. The hospital attendants took me to the operating room. I seriously thought I was gonna die. I had experienced four days of labor pain. I felt like the doctors were conspiring with my family, trying to teach me a lesson. I knew I was not going to have another baby anytime soon. I even told the doctor to kill me and let the baby live. His name was Dr. Fear. I couldn't believe it. What a name? He said to me, "This is not Little House on the Prairie. You are going to have this baby."

The nurses were all betting on my baby's weight and length. They were having a good time with my pregnancy. Shavon was the only baby born at Southampton Hospital that night, April 16, 1989. I had my baby. I started enjoying every bit of her. Because we spent so much time together, we were so close. It was difficult to get away from her and even more abstruse to find a babysitter. Even until this day, she is extremely close to me.

Affection is needed in families today more than ever. At least, that's how I feel. I say this because even though I adored my daughter, I wasn't always as affectionate as I am today. I had to fight through the pain to get to where I am today. Because of these earlier experiences, I didn't know how to show affection. I was still battling relationships. I didn't want to get to close and allow anyone, including my children, to get to close to me. I was sick on another level.

I emulated my mother's lack of affection and her indescribable scorn with my first daughter, Shavon. She resented my lack of affection and coldness toward her for many years. It took years for her to heal from my lack of affection. She had counseling, many tough experiences, a few toxic friendships, and a couple of not so good relationships before she began to understand that perhaps the lack of affection in our family might be hereditary and perhaps an emotional or psychological disease.

Now, I know the cure. It's called, "Just Do It! Love on Everybody," even when it feels uncomfortable. It was normal to love, to care! It was not normal to be cold and unemotional which I had inherited from my ancestors, once upon a time.

Grandchildren

In life, I strongly believe, we received what we need most. My daughter was blessed with three of the most affectionate little people in the entire world. Seriously! Jaylen and Jeremy, my grandsons, tells us they love us all the time, especially when we were riding in the car, watching a movie, eating a meal, or relaxing. These moments are extra special to us because they happen when we least expect them, and "boy does that feel good." We love differently today because of the love they constantly share with us. I wish everyone could experience these happy moments with us.

Jaylen and Jeremy, hug and kiss me as soon as they see me. To hear them say grandma is the sweetest words ever. Love flows through their eyes and warms my heart when they call me grandma. It's contagious! My grandsons tell me they love me when I least expect it, and it makes me feel so good. The affection they have for each other is breath taking.

My granddaughter, Cyia, although very young, is the sweetest little baby I know. I see love all over her. I say this because we, my immediate family, healed the emotional disease of the family in which we came from. We learned that saying I love you, caring for each other, sharing with each other, kissing each other, encouraging each other, being there for each other, and even hugging each other is normal. Affection is accepted and appreciated in our family NOW. To be any other way, TO US, is abnormal.

"Although, my struggles continued while in college and during my pregnancy, I was blessed with my children's father's grandmother, my midwife, nurses, and doctors who I consider my Angels."

> "Our financial conditions became unsettling; we often missed payments, and at times, we barely could feed my daughter and myself."

Education, Marriage, and Work

College Graduation

FOLLOWING THE BIRTH of Shavon, I earned my college degree. I believe I was the first female at LIU South Hampton Campus to earn a BA in Communications and Advertising and Public Relations. I minored in Education. I accomplished those activities while I was pregnant, working several jobs and attending three colleges at one time. I received my higher education degree plus extra credits in three years. I was so proud of me.

I told my family I was graduating. I invited them to attend and celebrate with me. Did they show up for my graduation ceremony? No, they did not come. Shavon, my eldest daughter attended; no one else from my side of the family attended my graduation, just my new born baby who was to young to understand the significance and importance of this event for me. She sat in her red stroller with the blue fringe on top and watched, watched the ceremony, watched me march across the stage to receive my first college degree.

Her presence meant everything to me. To me, Shavon and I, graduated together. She was my wind beneath my wings; she kept me airborne, flying to greater heights than I had ever anticipated. Surely, she became my first biological angel.

My daughter's father's family showed up big for me that day. I was so grateful for their support. I am so appreciative of them for providing the needed support for me during that period. I will never forget the role they played in helping me during that very tough time. I wanted to enter my career field upon graduation, but before beginning my professional field, I got married.

Marriage

Parents have amazing influence on their children. I believed my grandmother was always right in her approach to everything. So, in marriage, I heeded her voice.

My grandmother told me, "Whoever you get pregnant by, you should marry that person if you are not married already." Because I did it a bit backwards, I decided to make it right as she mentioned years prior. I married because I felt it was the right thing to do.

Yet, I believe it's because of preconceptions that I got married in the first place. My grandmother shot straight from the hip. She opposed premarital sex but insisted on marriage if pregnancy resulted. She told me just like it was. I tried to do what I was taught to do; I trusted my grandmother even after her death. I got married July 14, 1989.

I remember that day like it was yesterday. I wore a little frilly peach dress with a big bow attached to one side. I had a saffron colored flower in my hair.

My little girl was at the ceremony too. Shavon was 4 months old at the time I married her father. She wore a pretty little pink and white laced dress. She looked adorable.

I was 20 years old at the time. A few of my family members came to support me. One of my uncles whom I adore to this day, he has always supported me. There I was again somewhat alone.

Some of my relatives didn't come because they did not agree with or approve of the marriage for their own personal reasons. They felt that it would not work because I had ambition, but my future husband did not. They felt we were unevenly yoked. His mother opposed our marriage from the beginning. She was totally against it. She said, "We would never have her blessings."

We went against them all and married anyway.

Within months of graduating from college, I was on my way to Washington State to be with my new husband who was still in the military. Shavon and I found ourselves spending a lot of time together. I knew no one. Sometimes my husband would go out in the field for 30 days at a time. I had to make things happen because we had few resources, just starting out as husband and wife.

Twice, the Army forgot to pay my husband. We fail behind in our bill payments and financial obligations. Several times, we did not have money to buy pampers for my daughter, leaving her soaking wet. I did not have a job nor money to ameliorate the uncomfortable condition which I found myself.

I took a chance and did something I had never done before, nor since that time. I went to the local grocery store and opened a pack of pampers and changed my daughter right then and there. I reverted to using cloth diapers until I could do better — sometimes sanitized cleaning rags, boiled in hot water, helped.

I did a lot of things I was not proud of to get by. I share it because I know that some people are having similar experiences if not the same. I remember filling my pockets with dry beans, so I could make a meal for myself. It wasn't always easy, but we got through those tough times every single time.

I remember one of those times we had very little food. My husband was in the field, again, and I was home alone with my daughter, without resources, without a means of securing money for Shavon and me.

I had no way to communicate with him. Because I was a new army wife, I didn't know who to call to solicit help. I didn't know one person in the entire state, not even neighbors.

What did I do? I took some of my husband's personal memorabilia which he had stored away and drove around town to try and sell them. I got lucky — I found a buyer. I got enough money to buy food and pay a few bills.

Selling my husband's personal belongings wasn't a clever idea. When he found out that I had sold his Army equipment, we returned to the place where I had sold his goods. He demanded them back from the people I had sold them to. They obliged. I didn't realize how valuable that stuff was. That was a learning experience.

Our financial conditions became unsettling; we often missed payments, and at times, we barely could feed my daughter and me. With the help from several military programs, we made it through. They donated food every week. This was an immense help.

I experienced a lot of negative events in my previous marriage when we lived in Washington State that made me question my grandmother's advice about marrying someone just because I was pregnant by that person. Let's just say, I had grounds for divorce during the first year of my marriage, yet I stayed the course for over 20 years.

People often asked me why I stayed so long to a verbally abusive husband. My answer was simple, "I stayed for the children." I was a very unhappy woman. I was miserable. I mentally prepared myself to accept the situation until death did us part. I was tired. I was getting mentally ill. My marriage was taking a serious toll on my health.

At times, I was ready to call it quits. I don't know how many times, to many times to remember a definite count. Every time I was close to filing for divorce, I heard my grandmother's words constantly popping in my head, "Marriage is for life." She believed that marriage was a long-term commitment. "Stick with your man no matter what," She said, "Never let another woman come between you and your family, fight for your family." I did just that. I was mad as hell, but I stayed.

Sales

While I was in Washington State, long before I became a teacher, I had a neighbor that lived downstairs in our apartment complex. She was very nice. She shared her knowledge freely. We talked often, about anything that was of interest to us, personal and professional topics. I felt comfortable sharing my problems with her. She was like a surrogate mother to me.

She introduced me to a friend of hers. This woman was a Mary Kay sales director. The directress was well dressed. She smelled good, and she looked good. I could see she was successful. After visiting her home, I knew this woman made money selling Mary Kay products. At the time, I was financially crippled; I couldn't buy a brochure.

My neighbor helped me to get started. I was 20 years old at the time. I tried to grow that business, but it was not my time. I didn't know what I was doing, and honestly my neighbor didn't either. Because I did so many facials, I learned how to travel around my new town a bit. That was a good thing. But, I still felt like I was wasting too much time. I hardly sold products.

I was working day and night trying hard to make sales. I did okay. Doing okay wasn't paying the bills or buying food. Doing okay wasn't good enough!

Fear set in, and I decided to get out while I was ahead. For the first time, I was afraid of failing. I decided to quit before I failed. This became a part of my new norm. Every time I got involved in anything that challenged me; I would quit before I failed. I would stop before I was embarrassed or ashamed. I would concede the race before I was announced the 2nd runner-up etc....

Even if I felt like I couldn't win, I would quit. I had to overcome this crepehanger mentality, and I did. I learned that there is no such thing as failure. There is a such thing as results. If failure is another word for results and you don't like the result, then change.

I always knew if I ever got this MLM thing down, I could become wealthy. I needed more Angels!

When I saw my Mary Kay business wasn't moving as fast as I wanted it to go, I applied for a job at a nearby nursing home in Tacoma, Washington. I was hired. My employer trained me to become a Certified Nursing Assistant (CNA). That was some experience. Although I loved the job, it was toilsome, fastidious, punctilious.

On the other hand, because I had a very strong love for the elderly, I discovered working with older-aged patients was easy for me. However, I disliked coming to work and being met with all kinds of troublesome situations. After a while the job became an abhorrent; I resented coming to work, finding my patients dirty and uncleaned, etc....

Although the job became displeasing, I enjoyed caring for my patients, often shopping for them to meet their personal needs: shampoo, shower gel, powder, and Vaseline. I cared for each patient daily, one by one, well into every night. I bathed and powdered their bodies, moisturized their skin, greased their feet, and put Vaseline on their lips.

When my work day ended, my patients were nice and clean. They loved to see me coming. I loved being there to help them. I had patients that would attempt to physically harm other patients. One lady attacked me because I asked her to take her medication. I was injured and out of work for two weeks. I was 20 and she was in her 70's. She was stronger than me. This woman had the strength of Samson.

Some patients had bowel movements and threw excrement at me when I entered their room. Another patient had a bowel movement and wiped the excreta all over the walls. I had a patient that was an ex-stripper who often thought she was still working. She would take off all her clothes in the hallway and entertained the men. They loved it, but I sure didn't. Whenever I heard my name announced over the loud speaker, I knew exactly who the patient was and what he or she needed or had to have done. Even though the job was at times troublesome and arduous, it paid the bills. I was beginning to live.

> "Some patients had bowel movements and threw excrement at me when I entered their room."

Teaching

We eventually moved from Washington State to New York. We stayed with several of my husband's family members until we rented a place of our own. Moving back to New

York was an exciting time for me yet demanding and vexatious.

Well it was time for me to make my degree work for me. Teaching was my major career focus. First, I got a job working in the grocery store. Later, I applied for a teaching job in Brooklyn, NY. After waiting several tense minutes following the interview, I was hired as an elementary school teacher. Now starting a career as a teacher, I was so elated, knowing I might be in a better position to solve some of my past financial problems.

I followed my grandmother's advice again. I wanted to make her proud even though she was deceased. I taught nine years at St. Marks Lutheran School in Brooklyn NY. For once in my life, I had a guaranteed paycheck with benefits. I had just crossed the threshold into another phase of my life while continuing to integrate my professional and personal demands into positive experiences: advanced postsecondary courses, teaching, marriage, daughter, along with acquiring my own personal freedom for the first time in my life. At least that's what I thought.

Even though I was teaching, I realized early on that the education profession was not going to be sufficient to meet my family's needs. I was not earning enough money; we were living from the proverbial, "paycheck — to — paycheck." We needed more revenue and less expenses. I had to wait two paychecks before I could pay my rent.

I decided upon an alternate plan. I decided to add business sales to my repertoire of professional skills even though I had little knowledge of the theory or process of sales other than my brief flirtation of selling Mary Kay products in

Washington. I proceeded to the wholesalers in Manhattan and purchased hair accessories, stockings, hats, scarves, socks etc..., anything worth selling, novelty items initially. My customer base consisted primarily of my co-workers and friends. When they didn't have the money, I would still sell to them. I knew I would collect the money on payday. I kept an on-going tab and ledger of who purchased, what they purchased, how much they paid, and how much they owed me on payday.

I became even more creative. I made homemade cakes and pies. I took orders and even sold slices when plausible. Our family needed money, and I was committed to earn enough "greenbacks" to cover our rent and bills. In each pay period because of the extra money I made, I made it happen; bills were paid on time, and we had sufficient food to eat.

I believed in myself—I always knew that working for myself was the way to go. I continued to possess this mindset through the years. Selling was a method to accomplish our family's priorities, and it allowed me to make ends meet. Finally, I was proud of me. My sells skills and my "I can do it spirit" grew stronger every day. My coworkers looked forward to the little deals I would conjure up weekly before payday. I realized that I was accomplishing one of the basic tenants of sells — fill a void by creating products to meet individual desires. I helped them to fulfill their desires; they helped me to meet my needs.

From my initial beginnings of selling products to my co-workers and friends, I entertained venturing into more professional sales approaches while still holding down a steady teaching job. Muti-Level Marketing was the sells prize

I sought even though my first serious Muti-Level Marketing experience with Mary Kay was rather disquieting.

When I started teaching, I felt like my degree was going to finally get a workout. Because I was teaching, my daughter could attend a private school free of charge. That was a load off my shoulders. Shavon started PreK when she was 2 years old. She was one smart cookie.

"Although, my struggles continued during my marriage, I was blessed with friends and co-workers who I consider my Angels."

Damian—
My Second Born

MORE TRIALS AND tribulations came my way when I least
expected it. Understand, it took me 11 years to pay
off my college loans. I didn't want my children to go
through that. I assumed they would not get scholarships.
That was negative thinking. I always assumed they would
have to pay for their college education like I did. I figured
spacing them out would be the way to go. I didn't want to be
faced with paying double or triple tuition at the same time. I
figured while one would be in college, the other would be in
high school and so forth. I figured that when one graduated
from college, the other one would be entering. I had what I
thought was a very good plan.

I did not want to have my children back — to — back like my grandmother or my great grandmother did. My husband and I practiced family planning. Shavon was three years old, and I was ready to have my second child. I became pregnant again right on schedule. Having my children four years apart was ideal to me.

Now I was pregnant again. This happened just as planned. We were on schedule. We discovered that we were having a healthy boy. In my head, I was doing everything right. After all, my grandmother had 11 healthy children; her mother had 11 healthy children, and her friend had 26 healthy children. These women had no hospitals, no medications, etc., yet all of their children were born healthy.

Having a mentally delayed child was the furthest thing from my mind. I assumed the best, never thinking the outcome could be different. What could go wrong?

My son's due date was scheduled between late December 1992 and early January 1993. On January 1, 1993, my water broke. Because I had never experienced this before, I assumed the water that was leaking from my body was due to a very weak bladder. I thought the baby was laying on my bladder and causing me to wet myself.

The contractions started. When I got to the hospital, they did a sonogram. At that time, they noticed I only had 1 cm of water in my womb with my baby. I was in labor with him for 18 hours. Every time I had a contraction it would squeeze the baby and take his breath away causing him to not be breath properly. Because I was almost fully dilated, the doctor decided to wait until I was fully dilated, so I could have my baby vaginally. I was very dry, the doctor had to use forceps to help me give birth to my son.

When Damian Jr. was born, one of the nurses in the recovery room informed me to ask the doctor what was wrong with my son. She saw there was something wrong. I assumed because she had helped deliver and cared for so many new born babies, she knew something wasn't right. Soon after my son's birth, several doctors came into my room to tell me that my son had lost oxygen. They said we should be prepared. My son may never walk, talk, feed himself, go to the bathroom etc... I didn't want to hear that and neither did his father. His father ran them out of the room.

All I could do was what I knew how to do and that was pray. The doctors labeled him as a child that would be severely mentally retarded. Not only did he lose oxygen, but his urethra did not develop all the way. Because of this, my son had to undergo several operations to correct his urethra. One of the operations was six hours long because they had to take skin from one part of his body to use it to rebuild his urethra. Damian Jr. suffered immensely.

"Although, my struggles continued during my second pregnancy, I was blessed with nurses and a son who I consider my Angels."

> "I was perplexed: I didn't want people to discover what I was doing because I falsely concluded it was beneath me to do this sort a thing with a college degree."

Mary Kay Sells Again

DURING THIS TIME, I continued to teach. I had a job that had my name written all over it. My plan prior to my son was to work for 25 years then retire, so I could live happily ever after; however, now I had a child that really needed me. He was my second biological angel. What was I going to do?

I had to make a major life changing decision. Should I keep working and retire after 25 years like grandma commanded, or should I find another opportunity to generate income, so I would be able to focus on my son more often? I started to think about other career options; network marketing came to mind.

> "I was okay with being broke. I had become accustomed to that."

I remembered the very successful Mary Kay sales director from Washington state. By surprise, I was invited to a Mary Kay meeting. I went. I was shocked. I had never gone to a network marketing meeting. This was over the top as far as I was concerned. Women looked good and they smelled good. They were all dressed up and made up. They looked like dolls. They were all smiling and laughing. Everyone was super excited. They were hugging each other and kissing each other like they were family.

I sat in the back quiet as a lamb. I didn't want anyone to notice me. When it was time for the meeting to start, everyone jumped up and started singing a song. It went like this: "I got that Mary Kay enthusiasm up in my head, up in my head, up in my head. I got that Mary Kay enthusiasm up in my head, up in my head to stay and I'm so happy so very happy," and so on. They were making gestures to go with the song, touching their heads and all. I couldn't believe what was going on.

All I knew was that I needed some of that in my life. I wanted to make money, but I wanted the recognition more than anything. I wanted to feel appreciated. When I was growing up, my faults were always the center of all conversations, and I was constantly reminded of all the things I did wrong. When I did something good, which I tried to do often, it went unnoticed or was simply ignored. I tried to get positive feedback. That was like pulling my wisdom tooth on my own — not easy, painful at best.

I joined Mary Kay and went to work. Whatever the director asked us to do, I did that and more. I took on every challenge that was given. For me, I needed money, but I needed another means to help my son. I was okay with being broke, temporarily. I had become accustomed to that. If I had enough to take care of myself and my family, I was fine with that. For me, it was about getting the hugs and the kisses for doing an excellent job while appropriating more time to be with my children.

One day, I was on my way to a sell's meeting, and I realized that I needed a guest, and I didn't have one. I saw this woman walking down the street. I pulled up to her in my new Mary Kay car. I said, "Ms. I am going to a meeting, and I need a guest, will you go with me." She said, "I don't know you." I said, "I know but this would really help me if you came." She started walking off. I said, "Ms. I am a Christian; I love the Lord. I won't bother you. I just need your help." The stranger got into the car with me. I said to myself. If that was all it took, I was going to do that repeatedly. That was my first and last time. My peers thought I had lost my mind. I was on a mission for me. I needed healing and I was going to get it one way or the other.

When my guest and I reached the meeting location, I had the waiter put her meat, that she had in her bags, in the freezer. She sat through the meeting with me. I received my recognition, appreciation, hugs, and kisses. It was all worth it.

I think; therefore, I had become one of the top encouragers in my family. I knew what I felt like without it and I knew how I performed with it. As a result, the rewards that followed were amazing. I won my first car after four months of being in the business. I became a director in record time and went on to win my pink Cadillac. This was my first real taste of network marketing. It became my therapy. I was perplexed: I didn't want people to discover what I was doing because I falsely concluded it was beneath me to do this sort a thing with a college degree. That was dumb thinking on my part. I didn't know that it was the second highest paid professional sells position in the world with real estate at the time being the highest paid sells profession.

Think about it, how many times did I hear, go get a real job. Please, I had a real job, and I was glad I woke up because of my son. I thank Jehovah God for Damian Vincent Colon Jr.

"Although, my struggles continued while I taught school, I was blessed with a second job selling Mary Kay products and meeting new friends who I consider my Angels."

> "I had to conquer the demons inside me that were causing me at times to hate my situation to hate my life, to hate my son's illness, and at times to hate my son, and myself."

Transition

Leaving the Teaching Profession

I DECIDED TO LEAVE teaching: resigning was not an easy decision; I was poised to lose a lot. I gave up my benefits, a guaranteed paycheck, my summer months and holidays off, free schooling for my daughter, and much more. Yet, at this point, I didn't care; I became incensed with the school administration that forced me to comply with situations which required me to secure their permission to leave the school early or arrive later to tend to Damian's doctor's appointments or his health issues.

It was a struggle to get those who were in authority to understand my situation. It was like they didn't care. One day I needed to leave. I was told no because I had a class.

That was it for me, time to walk away, time to take a chance on me, time to handle my personal affairs without having to gain someone else's approval. I knew somewhere deep inside of me that I could do it if I reached back and grabbed that burning desire I had when I had to get my four — year degree in three years. I resigned, and I never looked back. I did not regret my decision. Taking a chance on me was worth it because how could I let myself down. Right?

Damian Enters School

For a very long time I shielded my son. I was very protective of him. It took years before I could openly talk about my son and his health challenges. I locked a lot of emotional guilt and tension inside. I didn't want to be judged, and I didn't want him to be judged or even made to feel uncomfortable or made fun of. This was my baby, and I owed it to him to protect him.

Think about it, I planned that pregnancy. I literally waited to get pregnant and give birth to a second child in four years following the birth of my first child. Imagine, finally getting pregnant right on schedule and within 24 hours, I was told I would have to take care of my child for the rest of his life because he had a physical ailment. Man, I was done. I thought to myself, what could happen worse than this? I did not realize to later that my son's health issues became a blessing in disguise. I just couldn't see the sun for the clouds.

My son started attending special needs (early intervention) schools before he was two years old. He was in diapers until he was 11 years old. His diapers were delivered to us once a month by UPS. Sometimes they were orange and other times they were green. It was not a comfortable time for me or my son. People showed their true colors during this time as well. It was not easy raising a child that was developmentally delayed. At times, I felt all alone, again. Sometimes I felt cursed. I was back to feeling helpless all over again. I had a special needs child; I needed a break. I needed time for myself. I was beginning to burn myself out.

Damian's Health Challenges

I asked a few family members for help with my children. They told me that they would watch Shavon but not Damian. They told me Damian was too much to handle. I had two aunts that bent over backwards to help me. One passed on and the other stayed with me for years, and she helped me get on my feet. My aunt Elouise believed in me enough to come and stay and help me with my son. I will forever be grateful for the love that she showed towards my family and especially Damian Jr.

Early on, I had to deal with my son on my own. I remember being in church, the grocery store, restaurant, just about everywhere a person could imagine, not once but on several occasions, my son had a bowel movement. I had to handle the situation wherever it presented itself. I became weak and tired. It was getting harder and harder the older he got.

Imagine leaving a child with someone who agreed to watch after him then upon returning home I would discover that my child was still in the same diaper I left him in hours before. He had many urinary tract infections because he was left in soiled diapers by relatives and friends who failed to care for him.

I hated when Damian would get sick because he couldn't communicate his feelings to us. We had to often guess or rely on doctors to discover the issue. Sometimes he was misdiagnosed, and sometimes he would be sick, and we didn't know it. We have heard numerous times, it was a good thing I got him to a doctor before he became deathly ill. God was truly on our side.

Some of the same people who treated him so well when I was present were the same people who refused to change his diaper when I wasn't around.

I always felt that some of my son's close relatives had major issues with his disability. They would treat him one way when I was present and another way when I wasn't.

I knew people in my church had issues with Damian's disability also. Some of the church folks seemed to have been the worse. I'm not knocking church people. I am just saying that the ones I was around didn't treat my son well in my absence.

I knew who the people were that mistreated Damian because of his reaction to them. Sometimes children would make fun of Damian. They would laugh at him and mistreat him. Damian has a pure heart, and he loves unconditionally. It doesn't matter how people treat him, he will always be nice to them. I love my son.

Although Damian experienced many adverse experiences with other people while growing up, he would stay away from negative people. That much he did know how to do.

Damian had and still has a very high tolerance for pain. I had to guess if he was in pain. Once, I remember; Damian used the bathroom. He forgot to flush the toilet. This was one time I was glad he did forget. When I looked in the toilet, I noticed it was blood in the water. His urine also smelled strong. The odor was one that I was very familiar to me. I knew Damian had a urinary tract infection. He had several in the past. This one was different because blood was in the toilet, and the smell of his urine was extremely strong. I wasted no time.

Off to the hospital we went. What I learned next blew my mind. Upon arriving at the hospital, the doctors saw him right away. The doctors were surprised at how well Damian dealt with pain. They said that was the worse urinary tract infection they had seen. They commended me for getting him to the hospital when I did rather than waiting. They didn't understand how he dealt with the pain. I wouldn't wish this on anyone.

My son has been nonverbal since his inception. Specifically, at restaurants, the waiter/waitress often would ask my child what he wanted to drink or eat. Damian did not respond; he stared at them, but he would not say a word. He wanted to answer but couldn't. Sometimes Damian would just sit there, and the tears would fall from his eyes. I wished so many times he would someday be able to express himself. I hated seeing him go through the stress of not being able to communicate. I had to assume most of the time what Damian wanted to eat, drink, wear, go, do etc.... I had to learn how to read his body language and a little sign language as well. This was our way of communicating with each other for years. This was a trying time for both of us. It's gotten so much better over time.

Since his birth, I have been on a mission to help my son. I knew he wanted to do more for himself. Damian watched his baby sister and his nephews grow up talking, walking etc.... They all grew up before his eyes, and he noticed they were doing things he wanted to do. He just needed help putting it all together. Now, he watches Cyia, his niece. He adores her.

> "Since his birth, I have been on a mission to help my son."

In other instances, we often lost patience with Damian: we just didn't know what to do at times. Trying to help my son was very frustrating. We repeated ourselves many times to teach him basic skills before he comprehended what we were trying to communicate to him. Repetition became our best teaching method for my son.

It was frustrating to witness his failures at learning basic survival skills because we knew Damian wanted to do more for himself. Damian, just couldn't put it all together as quickly as he would have liked. When he accomplished something, he was excited, and he would smile broadly, lighting up the world.

He never got upset. He never got angry. Damian didn't have it in him then, and he doesn't have it in him now. He has been one hell of a child. I love him so much. He has meant the world to me. Most people who encountered my son did not really know him. I believed every human being can learn a lot from my son.

Damian is such a loving person; he just smiles, laughs, and looks at them. He doesn't care what clothes I buy him. He wears them graciously. He never asks for name brand clothes; he doesn't ask for money, he doesn't ask to go here or there, he only wants to be loved.

I know people would like to have healthy babies, men wanting healthy sons, sisters or brothers wanting healthy normal brothers or sisters, but I believed God gives us what we need and not what we want. Damian was what I needed. He changed my world for the best. Because of him, so many people have been touched in one way or the other. He has spread love. Because of the gift of Damian, I love better. I am a better person because of him also.

I assumed I would have another healthy baby. I never knew dreamt in a million years what happened to me would happen to me. I assumed that I would be like my grandmother, her mother and all the women that surrounded me who had only healthy children. I was never around mentally challenge people before I had my son. I saw them, but I distanced myself from them because I didn't understand.

Growing up in the South was quite interesting. Whenever young girls out of wedlock became pregnant, they were sent away to have their babies. When and if they returned, they returned alone. They had stretch marks but no baby. Having children out of wedlock were well kept secrets in our town. So many children who I grew up with in my home town thought the person they were living with was their biological mother or father etc... If they were lucky, they would find out who their real parents were before it was too late. A lot of people still don't know. This was the norm.

The perfect family didn't want any interruptions or any embarrassments. My grandmother was the opposite. If any of her children or grandchildren became pregnant, they had the baby and took care of the baby. She didn't care who saw or knew.

My grandfather took these situations seriously. He didn't like embarrassment and often talked about it. Two people two different opinions, I understood them both. I loved them both.

Conversely, growing up in the South, I witnessed women abort disabled children or allow someone else or some institution to care for the children. There was always that house on the hill that housed so called special people. Nobody wanted nothing to do with that house or those special people in it. I refused to give my son away. It wasn't in me to do that. The thought never crossed my mind. I stopped going to a hairdresser friend of mine because she asked me why did I keep my son. She said she would have put him away. Her opinion and comments turned me off so badly; I just couldn't patronize her any more. Somethings and some comments were better left unsaid. He was my disabled son, and I was fine with that. I didn't understand why he was given to me in the beginning, but boy do I understand it now.

I have learned so much from Damian Jr. I know now that my son was assigned to me on purpose by God. I was blessed with an angel. For a very long time, I didn't speak about my son in public. This was not good — my stress burgeoned by dead-bolting my feelings and thoughts inside, causing me to experience unparalleled emotional grief. I thought if people knew about my situation, they would judge me, make fun of me, and blame me for having a disabled son. I was psychologically and emotionally conflicted.

Confronting My Emotional and Psychological Demons

I had to conquer the demons inside me that were causing me at times to hate my situation to hate my life, to hate my son's illness, and at times to hate my son, and myself. Before long, I made a conscious decision to tackle my psychological trauma, deal with my son and his health issues, and confront my emotional derangement.

I noticed early on, the more I shared the more people cared. I was showered in love all the time. I started sharing my experience with others, friends, workers, and sometimes strangers. I needed answers, and I needed them quickly. I had no idea that answers would come from sharing my story which led me to tell my story here, hoping it will help others who have found themselves in similar situations.

This was the beginning of wonderful things to come. At the time, I didn't know that my son's disability would help me to heal. The more I shared my son's story, the better I felt. Communicating Damian's story to others also opened doors of opportunity, products, people, etc.... In fact, sells increased as I became more comfortable reporting my life to others publicly.

I am still so grateful for that love that was shown by other people I have met on this journey of life. It is exactly what I needed to feel better about him and myself. I began a process that was leading me to overcome self-indignation to emotional purgation that would aid me in my quest to help my son.

I took advantage of all the information that was shared with me. I didn't know that the world was loaded with tons of valuable information and products that could benefit my son and my family. At the same time, I was upset with myself for engaging in self-pity, shame, and doubt. I wasted so much time. I removed the greatest barriers to my son's growth and my success — my psychological and emotional scars which merely covered the pains and wounds but did not heal the injuries.

Because I was so desperate to help my son help himself, I allowed many people to recommend different solutions to my son's medical problems. I went on a serious mission. I tried some of everything that was suggested to me for him. He never acquiesced nor yielded to my experiments with him. He wanted to make a shift in his life as well. I knew he did because he responded to the trials and changes gracefully. I noticed his positive reactions; he was excited about the possible improved outcomes as well.

"Although, my struggles continued after exiting the teaching profession and entering sells full time, while watching my son advance, I was blessed with meeting new friends who I consider my Angels."

> "When I learned more about the roles acid and alkaline played in our general health, I decided to do better right away."

Revelation

Selling Alkaline Water Ionizers

WORKED IN A company several years ago. I had numerous business partners. One of my partners was attracted to my story. She heard me speak of my son and his medical problems on various occasions. Her heart was opened.

She called me one day and told me that she knew of a product that she thought might benefit my son. She said it was an innovative technology from Japan. She told me it costed about $4,000.00. Honestly, she told me too much. I had already made up my mind. I was not going to buy whatever it was she was speaking of.

After several invites, I only went to her house out of respect because she had mentioned my son, and I desired to solicit additional information about her network marketing background. She performed a Ph test on several clear beverages. Back in the day, we didn't have all the information available to us that others have today. The Ph test was all we did to demonstrate our product. Honestly, it was all I needed to make an intelligent, well informed, educated decision. Our previous conversation started to make perfect sense.

To my surprise, every beverage she tested (soda, bottle water, sports drinks, and tap water) all tested acidic. These were all beverages that I had been giving my son. I just didn't know what I didn't know. Even in college, during biology and chemistry classes, we didn't spend much time on alkalinity and acidity. I spent more time on alkalinity and acidity in cosmetology school to be honest. I was one of those parents that allowed my son to drink soda, sports drinks, bottled water, and tap water. I assumed the clearer the beverage the safer the beverage. To me, back then, color equaled sugar. I have since discovered differently.

I thought that all water was created equal. I felt that those who processed and treated drinking water wouldn't allow bottled water to be sold in stores if it was unsafe. I felt that tap water was 100 percent safe all the time. I was under the impression that tap water was new water. I didn't know we were using and drinking recycled sewage water.

I knew that my son's body was working overtime all day and night to neutralize acid that I had, not knowingly, been giving to him. His body was constantly fighting to stay in balance. Because his body was constantly fighting to maintain balance, when I gave him acidic foods and drinks, his body robbed itself of minerals from his organs and calcium from his bones to neutralize the acid.

Because of my lack of knowledge, I was destroying my own children. Also, I was destroying myself. Our body heals itself. We were designed in this manner. Water, pills, potions, etc…, did not heal my son. Those products did not provide the nutrients my son needed to improve his health. When I learned more about the roles acid and alkaline played in our general health, I decided to do better right away.

Essentially, my sponsor had introduced me to problems associated with drinking acidic beverages. Secondly, she demonstrated a machine that was connected to her very own faucet. She told me the filter removed lead, sediment, rust, odors, chlorine etc…. She said that it produced the highest grade of alkaline ionized water in the world. At the time, over 10 years ago, I didn't understand it all, I liked the way it sounded. The prospect of using a technology that was being used in Japan for over 40 years and was considered a medical device in Japan was exciting to me. I wanted to learn more. I researched the company's history; I began to appreciate the science and methodology behind alkaline, and its positive benefits to the human body.

I discovered that these machines were used in hospitals all over Japan for years. With that little bit of information and the information I could discern from other sources, I decided to purchase a machine that would enhance the quality of water my family and I would be drinking. I was excited. I reasoned that alkaline was the missing link in my son's medical regimen.

Because I was in a bad place money-wise, I had to use the companies in house financing program. The company allowed me to purchase my machine by making a down payment. At the time, they didn't require a credit check. I was excited about that. Had they checked my credit at the time, I would have been in trouble. Thank you!

I did not wait to purchase a machine that I believed would one day be beneficial to my son's health. I paid the price for the water ionizer: its performance and objectives made sense, so I took immediate action after witnessing the pH test. I began to implement the machine and its concomitant directions with my son immediately; results happened almost spontaneously. His body responded favorably to good clean healthy water.

In a few short days, I received the machine, set it up, and administered the water to my son. I joined in and began to drink the filtered ionized alkaline water myself. I noticed a change in my son's health almost immediately. I didn't make mention of it too soon to people. I honestly thought I was seeing things.

I noticed a change in my son's physical and facial features initially. Secondly, his cognitive orientation and thinking became clearer. He focused so much better.

Damian was doing a lot of things doctors predicted he would never do. Doctors had predicted that my child would be incapable of performing independently from us, based on their past experiences. Once upon a time, I believed all that was said to me when it pertained to my son. When I started believing in the power of my Creator and the effects of clean healthy alkaline ionized water, I started seeing results and changing my beliefs. The body really can heal itself once a person gives it the right tools to work with.

Prior to good, clean, healthy, alkaline ionized water, Damian learned everything through repetition. He was now able to put things together in his head in logical sequences within a specified time frame. He advanced from doing almost nothing for himself to accelerating his learning. Damian, after years of not being able to go to the bathroom by himself, now he began to use the restroom independently.

Today, he knows how to use a remote control, and he is an immense help when it comes to dressing himself and doing household chores. It was as though I cleaned up a dirty fish tank. After I changed the type of water my son and I were drinking, our bodies performed better, especially my son.

We can take a lot more abuse than fish, but we can only take but so much, too. I'm so glad I found out about alkaline ionized water when I did. I am not making medical claims; I am just excited about having the opportunity to help my body, my son, and daughters.

As time progressed, Damian's physical and mental faculties improved. He felt better about himself. He smiled more. He cried less often than he did in the past. He sang and danced his way to where he wanted to go. I am so grateful. I feel so blessed. I am so glad God created him for me. Damian has grown so much. I am so excited for him and his future.

Damian wasn't the only one that needed to change his water. I needed to change the type of water I drank, too. At the time, I was over-weight (almost 300 pounds), but I was not the least bit concerned about it.

I was satisfied with being very obese. I assumed because I was born and raised in the south and came from a real country family that was filled with big beautiful healthy women, I was just going be one of them. Also, I believed in the "big bone" myth. I was told all my life that I was big boned. I was not going to possess a small stature forever.

The day came, and it was like I blew up like a balloon over a few short years. I have erased and replaced those self-denigrating words because using the alkaline machine and resultant water, my life changed positively, also. I have lost over a hundred pounds as a result of giving my body what it needs and taking away the things that it doesn't.

I had to change all around. This was not a quick fix. I exercised more; I eat good carbs as much as possible; I eat lots of raw fruits and veggies, and I drink lots of healthy alkaline ionized water. Also, I ingested lots of turmeric/cur-cumin supplements from Japan. I replaced my toothpaste with 11.5 Ph water, and I rinse and gargle with 2.5 Ph water. I wash my clothes with 11.5 Ph water. I soak my fruit and vegetables (organic or not) in 11.5 Ph water.

I was surprised at the stuff that was washed away. I used the 6.0 Ph water to clean my skin and windows. I can go on and on. I had to experience to understand it all; I had to make more changes, but it was worth it from a health standpoint and a financial perspective. I have saved thousands of dollars over the years on toothpaste and washing detergent alone.

I don't know why some people fell off the proverbial cliff or failing to grab a limb to soften their fall. Either way, I paid then not later. Prevention was always better than cures. I decided to take a chance on me. Don't get me wrong, doctors have a necessary place in the medical community. I often said, "If I were to break my leg, don't bring me any alkaline ionized water. Please rush me to the doctor."

> "... using the alkaline machine and resultant water, my life changed positively ...."

Understanding that a doctor was one who practiced medicine, helped me to understand that there were no guarantees.

When I found something good for myself and my family, I added it to my health portfolio. I am not a person who had to seek permission from any health care professionals to take care of myself and my family. We always knew we had to take care of ourselves. If we did not, who was going do it for us? I learned a long time ago that how we treated our bodies would determine how we live out our lives here on earth and directly affect the outcome of our lives. Agree?

Alkaline Ionized Water

Even though, I wasn't looking for any benefit from changing my water, I received benefits anyway. From what I knew, boarder line anything opposite of good health was not good. I acted fast to deal with any incipient health issues.

Prevention became my cure. I decided to act. I begin to listen, read, and learn about healthy ways to improve me. I was so glad none of these illnesses ever became my reality. When I began to treat my body like I loved it and appreciated it, I experienced amazing results. When I began to listen to my true self and stop believing the myths that had haunted me for so many years, I started to see an enormous difference in me. My body taught me a thing or two.

Our bodies were made perfect in my opinion. We have destroyed its form and beauty by engaging in poor diets, increasing stress, and snowballing sedentary lifestyles. Our DNA has held in its memory positive health practices while directing old remedies and medical traditions that we acquired from our family members. We tried to forget it, but our DNA can't forget! It was designed that way.

I knew we needed to reunite our healthy past with our future. Our bodies tried to adjust to our food selections and lifestyles. Because of maintaining a healthy balance between foods and lifestyle, I dropped weight quickly. My body identified with good, clean, healthy alkaline ionized water: the same water I developed in and drank when I was a youngster. My waistline shrank as my body released waste. The acidic level in my body changed toward an alkaline direction, more neutral, causing me to release more toxins that impacted my weight and health. By eating the right selections of food, my body didn't have to work so hard to maintain balance. My active choices helped define who I have become today.

My body was finally getting proper hydration. My chapped lips became smoother; my fingers and toes no longer looked like prunes. My body rejuvenated itself when I started to hydrate properly (drinking half of my body weight in water daily). The taste of this clean alkaline ionized water seemed fresher and more fulfilling to my body. The more I drank, the more water I wanted. I was getting my sexy back, reinventing myself sort of speaking. I was no longer big boned (myth). Every day, I was becoming more satisfied with my body and mind. This was a few less things to stress about. Getter better and better all the time was my new theme.

When we started drinking alkaline ionized water, we didn't know much of anything about this new masterpiece of a machine. This type of technology was above our heads, seriously. We knew only how to press the 9.5 Ph button to retrieve the wonderful elixir of alkaline ionized water. When people asked for a glass of water, what did we do? We gave them all 9.5 Ph. The success stories of others who experienced drinking the new water started to figuratively pour in. This was a very interesting time for us all.

For many, the experience of drinking alkaline ionized water was unbelievable. For others, the change to alkaline ionized water happened to abruptly. I laughed but my health was not a funny matter 10 plus years ago.

People started detoxing themselves quickly. Initially, many users experienced diarrhea. Some had headaches, stomach aches to name just a few. We had no explanation at that time. We didn't know what we didn't know. We had it all so backwards in the beginning. People started detoxing themselves at breakneck speed. People were calling me asking me what I had given them to drink. Some people had back pains, knee pains, skin irritations, and more.

I told them it was just clean water. I told them to keep drinking the water; things would change and not to worry about the negative side effects. I assured them that their issues associated with them drinking the alkaline ionized water would soon pass. I knew this because I to experienced similar symptoms. They believed me, and they continued to drink the water.

I assured them that many of the issues which they were experiencing were common and they should not become overly alarmed. I really didn't know. I never focused on how important drinking clean water was because it never crossed my mind. I assumed that all water was clean. I trusted store brought water from shelves in local stores, and I trusted the tap water that flowed from the faucets in my house.

In the beginning, we heard everything — we were so misinformed..

We were told not to allow the beauty water to run through our machines because it would destroy the machine. Beauty water was forbidden in the United States and was only used in Japan. We were told not to use the electrolysis enhancer chamber because it was totally unnecessary and those who lived in America didn't need it.

The more 9.5 Ph water we gave to people, the more they wanted. The lines to my house started to get longer and longer. People always reported positive news. Their desire for the water increased, extremely. It was like they got a good water addition!

People liked the results then they purchased their machines. Some paid cash, and others selected the in-house financing program.

The activities described above began my adventure into selling alkaline ionized water machines. Little did I know I would become a multi-millionaire doing this. This technology has benefitted my family, my friends, and especially my son Damian. Damian does not drive a car, attend college, cook gourmet meals, nor wash his own clothes. However, he has progressed beyond belief, beyond doctors' expectations, beyond my postulations. Many families are happier today because we shared this information with them years ago. We still share today.

My son is on his way. I believe one day he will be able to do a lot more. It is already happening. It is a blessing to witness such happenings. The excitement for Alkaline ionized water still breathes today! People can't seem to get enough.

Because of the benefits that my son and I received, people became very interested in our technology. I started giving away even more water. People stopped making appointments to come and get water and started just showing up at my house. This quickly got out of control. I knew this had to be something powerful. I often felt like I was losing control. The crowds were sometimes a bit much.

A few acted like they owned my machine. People started referring other people. They told their friends that I was a nice lady that just wanted to give away water. This was not true. I am nice, but I had a family too; a family that needed to survive like other families.

I had to remind myself that I was not in the business of dispensing free water all day. My neighbors started asked questions. Even though I knew wasn't doing anything wrong, I was still nervous. I didn't know if it was legal to give away the water or not. Oh my! We were so lost back then. My water give-away strategy became a flag raiser, an unforeseen problem for me. It got worse! Without my permission, car loads of people visited and sat outside of my house in cars, some with tinted windows, and waited patiently for me to get home.

I realized quickly; I had a business that had taken a life of its own. It was breathing without life support. I changed my approach, and I started giving people a taste and a short trial. They had to decide to purchase or else the faucet would be cut off. In the beginning, I think I became fatigued easily after giving away water all day.

That was a job itself. Selling alkaline ionized water machines as a business opportunity was the furthest thing from my mind. I was not at all interested in doing business with the company or any other company for that matter. I was fine with where I was. Quiet as I thought it was kept, I was truly afraid of failing. To me, it didn't make sense to get involved early on because I felt strongly that people would not want to be associated with the company for several reasons. First, I felt that people would feel it was unnecessary. I was one who once believed that all water was created equal and assumed everyone else felt the same way. I believed that bottle water was a better option, but tap water was just as good. I felt that diet soda was the better soda because it had less syrup or sugar. I changed my mind. I still felt I would have to convince people and that would make it a hard product to market.

Second, I felt that most people would not buy the machine because of the cost of the product. I assumed a lot of people did not have the disposable income to purchase the machine, like I didn't. I felt this way because whenever I would ask some of these same people for a loan no matter how big or small they would always say, "We are out of money." I believed what I was told. They would complain about their finances all the time. To me, I was surrounded with broke people.

Boy was I wrong. In most cases, the individuals whom I thought would not buy a machine ultimately purchased one; however, those whom I thought would buy a machine did not purchase one. I found out rather quickly that people spend money on things they find value in. They discovered the money for purchasing when they were exposed to the value.

This is the reason many people don't succeed in business today. They believed that everyone thought and believed the way they thought and believed. I'm so glad everyone I had encountered didn't think the way I thought. This world would have been in serious trouble. I was one negative person spreading my negativity everywhere I went. I'm free of that thinking now. I am so grateful for that.

I was determined not to do the business. Once again, I didn't realize failure was my real reason for saying no. I didn't want to fail. I didn't want to embarrass myself. My sponsor continued to encourage me to take a position just in case I decided to build the business in the future.

It took some convincing, but I did it. I told her I didn't want to give anyone my social security number, like it really mattered. Trust me no one wanted my social security number back then. I didn't want it. That was just another one of my ways out. After a little back and forth about the social, she said, "What if that company shuts down?" She had me thinking about my personal situation and that company. I had the brains to know that timing in business was everything.

Although I was afraid to complete the paperwork to become a sale's agent for the company, I filled out all the forms, anyway. What if my sponsor was right? The more people drank the water and shared their stories with me the more I became interested in learning more about the technology that sat on my kitchen counter. I remember hearing these words repeatedly, "How can I get a machine? I need one of those! I want one of those!"

People started going against what I believed. They started buying machines. Some were paying cash. Some were going through the finance department. They were buying these machines!!!! The "negative me" still assumed this would be short lived. It was not something that was going to happen too often. I believed the buying spree was going to stop sooner than later. Man, I still can't believe how wrong I was. It gave me chills then, even now goosebumps flair on my arms when I think about the power of the water, excitement of the people, hope for my son.

From time to time, my sponsor called me and told me what was going on with my organization that she was building on my behalf. She always kept me in the loop. She was dreaming for me. She would get me excited. She knew if I were to become motivated, I would act. That's what leaders do. Right? They can't help but lead. Her technique was working. I couldn't sleep sometimes. I continued to sell an alarming number of machines. My clients were drinking clean healthy water, and they told others about their modern technology, and they to wanted to join the cavalcade of users after hearing all the good news.

People craved good clean healthy alkaline ionized water. Some acted like they couldn't live without it. When they would inquire about purchasing a machine or if they had questions that I couldn't answer, which was many, I pointed them in the direction of my sponsor. I gave them her address and phone number. She helped me close many sells.

She never turned any one away. She worked overtime. She believed in the product wholeheartedly. My prospects called her, made appointments, and scheduled meetings at her house. In turn, she performed demonstrations, answered their questions, helped them fill out the paper work and sponsored them under my ID number. She helped me close many sells. Who does that! That is why I love my sponsor. I will forever be grateful for Honor Wilshire. She is a real angel in my book!

When I really started working for the company, my mailbox turned into a manual ATM machine. I didn't pay much attention to the checks in the beginning. I just cashed them. I was at the 4th level when I stopped pointing my prospects in the direction of my sponsor and started working the business.

At the 4th level, I was getting paid 4 points per personal sale. That meant when I sold a machine that was $3,980.00, I would get paid 4 points. Each point for that technology was $285.00. I would make $1140.00 from one sale. I was motivated by two people, my best friend Yvette, and the other buyers were friends of a friend. Both families purchased machines around the same time and both paid cash. I received two checks on the same day. Those checks came up to almost $2,000.00. I say almost because they purchased smaller machines. That got my attention. I was financially strapped at the time, and receiving that money really helped my family out of some troubling times. I was super excited; I wanted to talk to everyone. That was a lot more money than what I was making with the other company.

My son was getting benefits; I was getting benefits; my friends were getting benefits. Something was right about this company. People were happy, healthy, and wealthy. I wanted some of that. I wanted it desperately.

I was with another company at the time, and the company was not doing well. They ran a promotion. I was one of the ones to achieve the goal, and they gave me the keys to a white Mercedes Benz. I thought I had arrived. I was addicted to that Benz. It was my first Benz, C Class model. I didn't care what kind of class it was as long as it was a Benz.

I thought that company would be around forever. I was so wrong. The writing was on the wall. Top leaders were leaving the company and pursuing other avenues of income. Tamia was determined to make it work. I looked forward to the challenge. I didn't know that the opportunity with the other company would soon end. They gave me a Benz, but the residual income I was making monthly wasn't enough for me to fill the tank with gas never mind helping me to maintain my lifestyle.

I got tired of running on their treadmill and decided it was time to get off and join Enagic. I was ready to make a move. However, I wanted to be certain this was the right move for me. Out of curiosity, I requested a downline report from the ionizer company. What I saw, blew me away. I had earned over $16,000.00 without even applying myself.

There was power in pointing. I thought to myself, what if I took the time to build the business. I decided to do just that. I started thinking about the future of my family. I knew if I kept on doing what I was doing with the other company, I was going to hit rock bottom again and again and again.

Having been there before, made me realize, I didn't want that for my family, myself, for anyone if I could help it. I took massive action. I called my sponsor and asked her to please allow me to come over to her house once more, so she could explain the business plan. I needed to understand how the company paid out this kind of money. I needed clarity.

I visited her at home, and she was ready for me. She had her dry erase board out and her markers. She explained as much as she understood. I got enough information to fly my plane. I didn't look back. My team and I were so busy; we didn't have time to look back. When I say we flew, it was an understatement?

From that month, August 2006, we started rocking and rolling. We held meetings in my car garage in Long Island. We grew fast: members of the team were often promoted weekly. We didn't quite understand everything, but we knew it was the best thing that ever happened to all of us, many of us today remain with the same company and are still using the same machines we purchased over 10 years ago.

What we did after that blew us away. We didn't know everything, but we knew enough to attract success. In the beginning, we didn't know other products existed. We didn't have brochures in English; all the promotional literature was written in Japanese.

The company did not have a company website. We had to really figure it out on our own. We focused on one machine. Imagine had we known the unknown. In a way, I am glad we didn't. The more people started to study and to learn about the business the more they wanted to teach. In many cases, incorrect information was given. Management had to come in and correct us. This was needed but took a lot of time.

Instead of sharing water and basic information, distributors started unloading advanced information (that they didn't even understand) and sells strategies (that none of us understood) to everyone they met. Sales increased at a rapid-fire rate. Ignorance on fire made us a lot of money. Maybe we need to go back to the old-time way. Back then it didn't pay to know everything. That hasn't changed!

I have a unique sponsor, and I am forever grateful to her. What she did for me was not normal in our industry, unfortunately. My sponsor thought enough of me, my family, my business partners, and my future to not only share with me but to encourage me to take a position in the company, so I would be able to share with others and be compensated. She was unselfish in her approach to help me. Thank you Honor!

Shantel — My Third Born

Shantel, my third born, I refer to her as my make-up baby. I had separated from her father for over a year. I was living in Brooklyn during this time. I had Shavon and Damian, living with me. When we decided to reconcile and try to make our marriage work, we moved to a mutual place in Queens. We got a storefront apartment on Rockaway Blvd in Queens, New York. Shortly after getting back together for the fourth or fifth time, I became pregnant with my baby girl, Shantel. She was a healthy bundle of joy. She was too cute to talk about and such a good baby.

I was 268 pounds When I had Shantel, my third child 16 years ago. I was a big one. I was big and beautiful not big and ugly. After all, I did know the difference. I was 32 pounds short of 300 pounds on a 5' feet 3" frame that I thought was big boned. That was just too much weight for me to be caring around PERIOD. My health was becoming a concern at the time. I was border line high blood pressure, diabetic, high cholesterol, and began to suffer from other ailments (aches and pains) as well.

"Although, my struggles continued while working two jobs, raising my children, and beginning to benefit from using alkaline ionized water, while watching my son continue to advance as a result of lifestyle changes, I was blessed with a mentor and my third child who I consider my Angels."

> "I learned that emotions
> and preconceptions truly
> can destroy a person if the
> individual allows it to happen."

Personal and Professional Changes

My Divorce

I'VE MET MANY people who divorced. As a result, their families were separated, and children were devastated. I witnessed parents trying to turn their own children against each other. Children took sides and turned against one parent over the other. I've seen it all. I remember when I made up my mind that divorce was the best thing for me. I sat my children down and told them what was going to happen. I didn't know my decision would be the beginning of a nightmare that would haunt me for years. It did. A lot lead up to my decision to divorce my husband. This was not an overnight decision. It wasn't a decision based solely on emotions. I felt the need to get out of my situation, and I did. Stress was mentally and physically taking a toll on my life. It was becoming a challenge to function on a day to day basis. I had had enough.

My divorce from my first husband was rather choleric which led me to make several ill-advised decisions. Arguments with my husband concerning communal properties — money specifically — became petulant. He assumed an intractable position to protect his interests, and I did likewise to protect my children, my business, and me.

I took a calculated risk and joined another company. I wish I hadn't done that. I knew why I was doing it, but I wasn't comfortable with my decision. I didn't feel like I could trust anyone enough to share the emotional tyranny which seemed to haunt me that stalked me like a wild beast. Betrayal was not an option; I could not trust any of my new colleagues with such personal issues which I was confronting.

To protect myself and the integrity of my family, I avoided talking about my personal issues, so I constructed an invisible wall around me that stopped others from entering and me from exiting my tattered emotional sanctuary. Again, I sequestered my fragile feelings and my present sense of hopelessness from others by keeping detached from co-workers.

To no avail, they still deduced my problem, uncovering my divorce proceedings, uncovering my pain. Details of the divorced they never knew, but I did not desire to shed more light on the issue with anyone. I came from the old school, never revealing problems in my household to others or the inner turmoil that wreaked havoc on my emotional state of being.

I endured; my divorce was needed for me to progress to the next level in my life. I sought peace and solace from my husband even if it meant being alone for the rest of my life. I accepted this predicament; I had faced this emotional roller coaster before — tarnished love with my mother — the lonely ride on the train to New York — child birth — raising a disabled son. I learned that emotions and preconceptions truly can destroy a person if the individual allows it to happen.

I was hurting emotionally and didn't know what to do. My divorce ended quickly, and I reengaged with my current business.

My husband and I grew separately, leading to a better life for both of us today. My children's father has been in their lives consistently. He has been an amazing person, and I wish him well in all his endeavors. We deserve happiness.

My CEO

During my divorce period, although I was a top leader, my income almost disappeared totally. My bank account went from thousands of dollars to $17.00. There were a few reasons this happened. The main reason was that someone reported me to the company. The person claimed that I was cross recruiting. The individual said I tried to solicit people from their group. This was far from true.

I received a lot of calls from people trying to recruit me into other businesses during that same time. I didn't report them. I still get many of those calls today. Every year, without fail, someone comes with the newest biggest most powerful amazing best money-making deal in the world. They make the grass look like gold with diamond flowers on the other side. My experience has been, "Don't let the bait fool you."

If I wanted to continue to swim, I avoided the worms, eschewed the bait and stay focused. When competitors wanted me, if they got me, they would have exposed me to the industry quickly.

Oh yes, word travels fast where we come from. Our industry of network marketing seems big, but it really is a small world. Most leaders know each other. If my name was out there, IT WOULD HAVE BEEN OUT THERE, and there is nothing anyone could do about it. I kept it clean. I kept my composure and integrity because my reputation was not worth any amount of money or fame in the world.

People deserved to make their own mistakes and decisions. Also, they deserved to earn a living to feed their families. I intended to be one who minded her business. I've never participated in the gossip game. That game has always been way too expensive for me to desire to play. I was taught to only say what I could repeat. I was taught to practice what I preached. I have done my best to do both.

I thought I knew who reported me. I never confronted the person. Some battles were better left alone. During this time in my life, I was growing so much; I didn't have the time or energy to fight in word, thought or deed. However, I eventually discovered the culprit who lied on me. Busy being about my business, I just avoided confrontation and acrimony. Time healed me emotionally. Remember, the battle was not ours.

It took me some time to heal. Because of this lie, I suffered quietly, again — concealing a scarred smile — cloaking the inner pain that continued to rupture my psyche. I never talked about it with distributors. I was always taught that good news swims and bad news drowns. I had trust issues, so I kept my mouth shut — locked next to my bottled-up emotions.

I went through real hell and back, unable to pay my life insurance — it lapsed; unable to take care of my children. My life and soul were in a deep pit of anxiety that finally surfaced when the CEO had one of his employees call and invite me to a private meeting with him, his wife, and a few others in Queens, New York. He displayed unreal compassion toward my situation. I often wondered how he knew about what I was going through.

He had been informed by someone in the organization. I tried to communicate with him on many occasions through a staff member or two only to get nowhere. Fate was on my side. Mr. Oshiro knew something was wrong. He has been a loyal friend, and I admire that about him. He saw and felt things just like I can. I admire him and respect him like a daughter would look up to her own father. I learned that he truly loves us and cares about us. He is an amazing CEO and leader.

I will never forget our conversation in Queens that night. I remember the moment when he asked me to tell him what was going on with me. I shared the uncut version with him. When I was done, he mentioned that I should have come and talked with him. Warmth bustled through my heart when he uttered those words. I felt helpless yet hopeful. My desire to do more became so strong. I wanted to help him in his business to help others. He unlatched the door that I had locked for so long; I felt relieved. I made a commitment that night that I would see his vision through, and I would play a major role in making it happen. I was committed. I still am.

Before I met with the CEO, because of all the drama, my picture was removed from the offices "Wall of Fame" by the request of distributors. My checks were put on hold, and I was removed from the leadership email list. I wasn't even invited to participate in any of the local meetings, seminars, super events, or anything. I felt betrayed, and at the same time, I felt that I had betrayed my business partners and my family.

I am sure, if I had spoken to the owner, before I made my decision, he would have helped me find a solution. Mr. Oshiro is one amazing human being. Our CEO rocked. We are so fortunate to have him as our true leader.

I regained my status in the organization, picked-up where I left off and business started to explode quickly. I fought for trust again. After I got the strength to share my reason for doing what I did, it became evident that I was not a bad person or a poor excuse for a leader. I just made a few bad choices.

I was back, and I was on my way to the top again. I shared my story on several live conference calls and at several live trainings. I used my firsthand experiences to empower others. My hope was to show others how to avoid some of the problems I had experienced. Not for nothing, but I've been in this industry a long time, 28 years.

I realized that it did not matter what business I was in or what I did; I still had to work but smarter. Why not be the best I could become. Character speaks louder than words, so I began to work towards self-improvement. I stayed focused and true to myself, my dreams, my ambitions, my goals. I began with a vow to finish what I started, by helping others to succeed by showing them correct ways of doing business. I started thinking about outcomes before I made any final decisions. These were just a few things I did to refocus my life through positive energy. I hope it helps you.

Avoiding the Scams

On three separate occasions while building my Enagic business I was approached and offered "The Next Big Deal," the deal of a life time, the biggest deal of all deals, the deal that was going to free us all by making us all super rich within hours, the deal that encouraged marketers to join and leave everyone else behind, the deal that was going to make me the company trainer and give me a $75,000.00 bonus or the biggest deal of all that was gonna help my son to be "normal."

For some reason, the idea of some company or someone helping my son always captured my attention. I was always on the hunt for the next "great product" that could help Damian Jr. I wanted Damian to succeed just as much as he wanted to succeed. For instance, a sells representative was looking for great leaders like me. He boasted, "We will put you on the phone with the owner."

"Alright now! The owner is going to speak with me."

The owner was always a God-fearing man on a mission to help people reach their goals. This may be true is some cases, but it sure wasn't true in none of my experiences. The owner paid leaders an upfront bonus of $10,000.00 or more per month to help them solicit other leaders from other companies. I call it GREEN GRASS talk.

The problem was once the leaders jumped the fence, they discovered the yard was full of holes, ditches, dead grass, weeds, rabbits, squirrels, raccoons, snakes, deer, etc.... They, the owners, all seemed to have an exit strategy. I didn't take it personal. I learned early on in my career, it was simply business as usual for some. For most leaders, when they left, they always came back. Some are still making their way back home. To avoid jumping back over the fence, I stayed put!

If I didn't stay focused, my peers would have started to question my integrity, possibly tarnishing my reputation. These were people who loved, trusted, and respected my abilities. "Jumping the Fence for other marketing positions was not respected and still are not today in our business. It led to distrust and double talk while producing few to little success. I remained faithful to my company; sometimes overlooking horrible comments, sly remarks, negative emails, text messages, social media drama or negative comments by persons not bold enough to say them face-to-face. It was simply not worth it.

Please, spare us all. Fly by night deals came around

"I never committed network marketing adultery."

at least once a month back then, even faster now. People made tons of money building businesses and shutting them down. They would launch a product with a quota in mind. Once that quota was met, it was exit time. It didn't take a rocket scientist to see the writing all over the network marketing walls. It was not about me. It was business as usual. My family was not factored into the plan and neither were my business partners. I Stay focused and loyal!

Money can be acquired in any business if the person stays committed and attentive long enough.

Never stop believing! Don't allow your fire to turn to ashes! I Kept the faith and maintained my integrity.

I learned never to trust money more than oneself. I never committed network marketing adultery. I chose to stay, never walking away. I did not drag other people down into a pitiless field of false dreams or uncertainty. We had no guarantees, and we all knew that. We sold proudly, no sham or lack of sleep at night because of business scams. My goal was to assist everyone and help them to grow. Greed never crossed my path; multi-level marketing was not a game. It was not a joke. For me, it was a way of life. Because I believed in it so much, I choose not to toy with another person's future. I took it seriously, and I still do today.

Every single time I turned away from my business, I regretted it. It was never worth it. Never! All the promises panned out to be a bunch of lies. I documented product failures, dishonest business partners, and corrupt compensation plans. They were all fake. It was time poorly spent, money wasted, and dreams put on hold when I attempted to turn away from my trusted business.

"Although, my struggles continued while working various jobs, raising my children, and training others in the alkaline ionized business, while overcoming problems on the job, I was blessed with a company owner who I consider my Angel."

> "The universe created this man for me: I am happier than I have ever been in my life."

Continuing to Grow

My Dear Friend

REMEMBER JENNIFER, WHOM I refer to as my big sister, telling me to write down everything I wanted in a partner, a husband, a male friend etc.... I couldn't really make sense of it then. I was still married to my first husband at the time. She thought if my first husband was the one, he would become what I wrote down, and if he wasn't, then whoever I created on that same piece of paper would one day appear!

Not long after I met Tony, I was cleaning out my closet. I found that piece of paper wrapped up inside of a pouch that looked all too familiar to me. It was the pouch that Jennifer had given me to put my dream man into. I opened it up and took the little piece of folded paper out. I began to unfold the paper, and to my surprise, all I could see was my Tony.

Imagine writing something on a piece of paper and throwing it in your closet and forgetting about it. That paper sat in that closet for over 10 years. I had cleaned that closet several times. I had given away tons of clothes from that same closet. I never came across that pouch until after Tony came into my life. That was a real moment for me. Everything that I had described that I wanted in a husband etc... was starring right back at me. In that moment, I believed! I was cold yet warm inside. The tears flowed down my face because for the first time I realized that I had gotten what I wanted, needed and deserved. I felt worthy and wanted.

Because I always trusted her advice, I just did it. Jennifer was there for me during those good and even more during the not so good times.

I remember her apartment was my outlet of peace. When I would call her late at night upset, she wouldn't hesitate to invite me and my children over to sleep on her pull out couch. We slept there a many of nights. The drive from Queens to Lexington Avenue in Brooklyn got shorter and shorter. Her son, my godson, DeAndre, was and still is a precious kind caring soul. He embraced my daughter, Shavon and my son, Damian, like they were his first cousins.

I recall not having any money several times and Jennifer gave DeAndre money to go to the Chinese restaurant to buy food for us all to share. He and Shavon walked to that Chinese restaurant a lot. I am just so grateful that people like this were placed in my life. All of them have played a tremendous role in who I have become today. I loved them deeply, like family.

Jennifer helped me grow up. I learned how to respect and appreciate money. I learned how to also say NO. She became my big sister. We became connected forever. I know she understands how we feel about her and how much she helped me and my family.

Tony, My Soulmate

My environment was not bringing out the best in me, so I changed it, so I could continue to grow personally and professionally. Trust me, I learned the ropes in more ways than one. Life was energy, shinning brighter and brighter, remaining in motion each day. I persevered; I did what I had to do to survive. I made immediate and direct changes; time did not hesitate or stop because I made some inappropriate decisions, along the way. Time kept moving: I did not waste it, anymore. I treated it like it was my last pay check.

The industry of MLM/Direct Sells has been good to me. My whole life has changed because of my decision to market Kangen Water Ionizers and do network marketing full time. In this life changing career, while on break during a business presentation, I met the love of my life, my husband, Anthony (Tony) Williams. I knew he was the one for me when he walked in the door. Don't ask me how I knew; I just knew. He was the only guest that showed up that night. He sat down, and I sat beside him. I started feeling funny inside, butterflies swarming in my stomach, fluttering about like a shy teenager.

I had this feeling of exaltation for that entire night. I kept asking myself if it was normal to be feeling this way so soon. After all, I had only been divorced for a little over a year. Then I realized that we often block our blessings by holding on to what wasn't assigned to us in the first place. I was reading the unseen and feeling the invisible. Tony and I getting together happened quickly, subconsciously, "a tout de suite."

I finally released my previous negative experiences with my ex-husband. My hands held someone else's hands: I was not only divorced but free! When I let go of my emotional fears, Tony appeared. After the meeting was over that night, Tony walked me to my car and handed me his business card. I drove home that night, thinking about him the entire drive home. When I arrived home, turning the key to my front door lock, I imagined coming home to him, unlocking the key to my heart.

I hinted to my daughter Shavon and my aunt Elouise that I had met someone, and I had a strange feeling in my belly. They laughed; they thought it was cute. I was nervous but ready to be all in. It just felt so right. This was a feeling I still can't explain. I asked my aunt if there was really a such thing as love at first sight. She said yes. She also said it doesn't happen for everybody. I considered myself very fortunate, special and blessed.

As I sat in the middle of my California King size bed, I could not help but dream about what life could be like. I texted him later that night. He texted me back right away. After texting back and forth for a while about sweet little nothings, the texting conversation got a little upfront. What he said to me next shocked me. He texted, "My blood takes you." I was like what in the world. What was the meaning, perhaps a vampire or blood sucker? Maybe this was all to good to be true. Maybe this was all too good to be true.

I didn't text him back for about an hour. Eventually, I texted back and asked him what did he mean by that. He told me he liked me a lot. It was like a breath of fresh air while waiting to exhale. I was so glad to hear that. I took off my armor and that was it. We started

> "He texted, 'My blood takes you.'"

going to business meetings together. Eventually, we added dinner to the equation, movies, shopping etc.... I felt like I had known him forever. It felt so natural. I knew he was the right one for me.

What a wonderful human being! I always wanted a partner who would be interested in working together and traveling together. I always wanted to partner with someone who was on the same page as me and who shared similar values. I got what I wanted and more.

Although he had been a plumber for more than 25 years, and he had his own plumbing business; he found time to help me do what I do. He was everything I ever wanted and dreamed of. When I designed my dream man on paper some 15 years ago, I had no idea he would step from the sheet of paper as I had described.

The universe created this man for me: I am happier than I have ever been in my life. I am truly grateful. We have hiccups here and there as we have grown together; yes, we do. Those minor issues have also brought us closer together every single time, maturing closer not apart. I loved him initially, from the beginning we clicked. What a sweetie? What I have admired about our relationship was our constant connection of working together and bringing out the best in each other.

We were not in competition with each other. We were not jealous of each other. Together was what we were and have become, like glue, binding our love forever and ever.

Tony and I exchanged wedding vows at Occasions Banquet Hall in Queens NY. Yvette Reeves, my best friend, presided over the occasion, along with, Jennifer Mahgoub, my big sister, and Chuckie Allen, my big brother on July 22, 2016. We had our public exchange of vows one year later, the exact same day in Glen Cove NY at the Glen Cove Mansion. That's a day I will never forget.

I became a better person as a result of meeting him. I have a life partner that I once only dreamed of — a life partner that was described on a piece of paper that sat silently awake in my closet for years.

We celebrated with over 200 guests. It was amazing. I felt like a Queen marrying her King. My mother in law, sister in law and brother in law came all the way from Trinidad to be a part of our special day. My uncle James Bethea walked me down the aisle. My aunt Elouise Bethea walked in place of my mother. My grandsons and granddaughter were in the wedding, too. My two daughters met me midway down the aisle and walked me the rest of the way to my husband, standing proudly at the altar. My son sat in the audience and enjoyed every bit of the ceremony.

We had family and friends come in from all over the USA and other countries.

On a special note, Mr. Isobe and his beautiful wife came from Tokyo, Japan to share this special day with us. To see the smile on my transformational coach's face, my mentor, Mr. Isobe, was a joy that I can't explain. He knew the latent strength in me from the first training I attended with him. He saw my transformation initially, and through the years, he watched me grow in the organization.

I am so grateful for him. I am not the same person I was before I met Mr. Isobe. It was as though, Mr. Oshiro sent him for me. I took his training serious and personal. I entered that room like a dry sponge and left filled with excitement and information.

Enagic sent us nine of the most beautiful flower stands I have ever seen in my entire life. Those flowers made our day extra special.

My Business

I want to also thank the CEO of our company. He has been in my opinion, a true example of leadership, a magnificent picture of health and strength yet humble. I have never met someone like him in all my years of being in network marketing. Because of his vision decades ago, I have been able to do things, go places, help people, contribute to changing lives, support my children and more. Most people have only dreamt of the lifestyle that most of us have been able to create as a result of embracing his vision. This was truly the best opportunity I have ever known of. He has contributed immensely to my financial and personal freedom — he has been in a class of his own. Thank you, Mr. and Mrs. Hironari Oshiro. I love you. We love you.

My Family and I

I got closer to some family and friends and further away from others, finally distancing myself from the negative ones. Because I changed, I inherited a new set of in-laws, family, friends, and an extended family. I have sisters and brothers now. I have more uncles and aunts than ever before.

Why has this happened? It happened because I grew and am still growing. I have grown out of relationships and have grown into new relationships.

I worry less now because I am on point. I have a mother, Patricia (Patsy) Checkley, who lives in Trinidad who I love and adore dearly. She has been such a wonderful person. I simply gravitated to her from the moment we met. I can call her and talk to her about anything and get sound mature advice.

She is not a sugar coater. She keeps it real all the time, and I appreciate that. I have learned so much from her. Whenever she's around, I just want to be around her, so I can listen learn. She has so much to offer and is eager to share it with anyone who will receive. She reminds me of my grandmother in so many ways. I cherish our relationship.

Maria Williams, my business mother, who has lived in Queens, New York for most of her life is another amazing woman in my life. She is from Trinidad also. She has blessed my life in more ways than one.

My aunt, Elouise, who lived with me for years, took on the role as mother, grandmother, and great-grandmother. As I stated earlier, she came to help me when I needed it most. She embraced me, my children, and my grandchildren as though we were all her very own. I don't know how I would ever be able to repay her. She has been nothing but good to me. I feel so special to have her in my life.

My life continues to get better because of the people who are in my life. I believe that if a person wants to surround themselves with good people with positive energy, good and positivity will follow them wherever they go. This has been true for me.

Since becoming self-employed over 24 years ago, I made many changes in my life. These changes have made me a better person, partner, niece, cousin, sister, mother, friend, aunt, grandmother, teacher, trainer, coach, speaker, wife, and more.

As I grew, I had outgrown others who were in my life in the past. The same people that were with me to help me get to where I progressed today, have remained faithful; however, others have fallen by the proverbial wasteland. Many friends changed as I succeeded. Often, I heard former friends say, "You are not the same. What happened to you?" My advice, I kept moving forward.

Because a person decides to follow this path doesn't mean his/her spouse, children, family, or even friends will support the business. Through it all, there were still people who saw something in me that I had not fully identified in myself. Understand, I was an emotional mess. I was figuring this all out the best way I could while on my journey. Now I understand that I went through it all for my son. I can now tell others what not to do.

I am so glad many of my friends, business partners and family did not give up on me. I am better today because I believed in my son, and he continued to believe in me.

Thank you, Leontine for not giving up on me and telling me what I needed to hear to wake me up. I will never forget you talking to me in the office, in the hallway, outside the door while I sat in my car. You saw what I could not see, and I am glad you did. You helped me to refocus on success and get back on track. I appreciate you!

I am very clear why God gave Damian to me. In my humble opinion, I believe my son was the main reason why our team grew the way it did as fast as it did in the beginning. My son's story inspired, encouraged, and helped so many people around the globe. I have gotten calls from as far as Africa and other parts of the world asking for advice regarding that special person in their lives. I hear from mothers, fathers, siblings, business partners all the time who reach out to me to talk about their how to deal with a special child or a special family member.

Lives have been impacted by my son's disability, all of the time, changing one at a time. This has been rewarding, making my heart smile. The door to hope for so many was opened because of my son's story and how that was given to me. My son, whom I once looked at as a burden, a set-back became one of our families' biggest blessings in disguise. His life helped me to gain financial freedom, health, peace of mind, and much more.

I don't think I would have found out about network marketing had it not been for my son. If he hadn't lost oxygen, I wouldn't have resigned from teaching. There would have been no need to resign. I would have worked for 25-30 years and retired instead. Our lives wouldn't have changed from a health standpoint or a financial standpoint. I wouldn't have met the many amazing people that I've met over the years. I wouldn't be where I am today for sure. I'm free because of my son. I am free because of the story that was given to me.

I am grateful that as a result of what happened to my son, people are able to grow through these difficult times knowing that there can be a positive outcome. Damian didn't suffer in vain. He came here the way he did to help others in his own special way. Because of my experience, I have learned to view every situation as a blessing.

You know, many people go to school, get good grades, get a good job all because somebody told them to do so. I was one of those people in every aspect of the word. I don't regret my life experiences because I learned from them all. As a result of all my stuff, my baggage, I helped others overcome their personal and professional burdens. Through my son, I helped others to heal. I am grateful for my life lessons.

Even though over the years I have been able to accomplish some things along the way, I still feel like my journey has just begun. I'm on phase two of many more phases. I'm not the same person I use to be. Because of my son, I became a certified motivational, speaker, trainer and coach with the John Maxwell Program. Because of my son, I became a member of the National Association of Professional Woman (NAPW). I am a Life Mastery Consultant with the Life

Mastery Institute with Mary Morrissey. Because of my son, my organization has grown significantly. Today our company has over one million users worldwide, and we are just getting started. Today our team has over 60,000 people using our products and sharing our devices worldwide, and I am happy.

"Although, my struggles continued while raising my children and dealing with family members, I was blessed with a soulmate who I consider my Angel."

Me

Tamia Bethea Williams

Born in Latta, South Carolina

Lives in Long Island NY

BA / Minored in Education, majored in Advertising and Public Relations

Licensed Cosmetologist

Master in Body & Brain Training

Lead Master Trainer for MLM — 3rd in the world to be promoted by top transformational trainer Mr. Isobe

Certified Lead Master Trainer for Enagic

Certified Motivational Speaker, Teacher, Trainer and Coach with the John Maxwell Group

Certified Life Mastery Consultant Specializing in transformational training — with Mary Morrissey www. tamiabetheawilliams.lifemasteryconsultant.com

Executive Member of the National Association of Professional Women

Full Time MLM for 25 years

Doing MLM for 29 years

Mother of 3

Grandmother of 3

Wife to a very handsome, spiritual, amazing man and soulmate Anthony Williams

Been with Enagic over 12 years

I have over 60,000 team members and a host of 6As, 6A2s, -2s and -3s

I am currently a 6A2-4, a top position in her MLM business.

I am the first female to make over a million dollars in Enagic and have made millions in the MLM industry. I create training materials, and I am writing my second book! My passion is helping people find their true selves — discover their purpose — and finish their journey with a bang! My favorite quote is, "Go through nothing but grow through everything!"

CPSIA information can be obtained
at www.ICGtesting.com
Printed in the USA
BVHW03s1519270318
511729BV00001B/1/P